What peo

<u>Breathe Bett</u>

By Jane M. Martin, BA, CRT
www.breathingbetterlivingwell.com

"You have done a wonderful job preserving the helpful experiences of some terrifically inspirational patients! This book would have been staggeringly important to us early on and will be to the patients, family, and friends who read it. I hope many patients will find this book, their reward will be a much better life, thanks to you."
Todd Pierce, husband of Mary Pierce,
Lung transplant recipient
St. Joseph, MI

"You have achieved the impossible! ...a book about sickness that is so good the reader can't put it down! ...a truly inspirational book!"
Jane Gillette, oxygen dependent person with COPD
Sacramento, CA

"_Breathe Better, Live in Wellness_ is a remarkable collection of writings based on personal experiences from individuals and family members of individuals with lung disease. This book offers patients and families a view of real world experiences, coping strategies and practical insights for successful living. For those of us [who] do not have lung problems _Breathe Better, Live in Wellness_ provides insights into the daily life of those [with chronic lung disease] and helps us to appreciate what we have."
Dr. Rick Carter, PhD, MBA
Professor of Medicine and Physiology
The University of Texas Health Center
Department of Medical Specialties
Center for Clinical Research, Tyler, TX

"Your book was really good. I think that everybody going through Pulmonary Rehab should read it before they start. They'd know what to expect and they'd get so much more out of it."
Ben Harris, person with COPD and Pulmonary Fibrosis

Breathe Better, Live in Wellness

Winning Your Battle Over Shortness of Breath

by
Jane M. Martin, BA, CRT

Foreword by Mary Burns, R.N., B.S.
Executive Vice President, Pulmonary Education and Research Foundation

ISBN 0-7414-1516-X

Published by:

Infinity Publishing.com
1094 New DeHaven Street
West Conshohocken, PA 19428
Info@buybooksontheweb.com
www.buybooksontheweb.com
Toll-free (877) BUY BOOK
Local Phone (610) 941-9999
Fax (610) 941-9959

Printed in the United States of America
Printed on Recycled Paper
Published January, 2005

Signed copies available only from the author. Jane may be reached at
<janemartin@breathingbetterlivingwell.com> or <jmartin@macatawa.org>
Please visit www.breathingbetterlivingwell.com
for more pulmonary information
and / or to order books through the publisher

This book is dedicated to the people who, while struggling day-to-day with the basic life-sustaining act of breathing, are able to live full and joyful lives. Our beloved friends with Chronic Pulmonary Disease can learn much from physicians and health care professionals, but they can teach each other as well. Most importantly, they teach us all so much about living.

❧ A MESSAGE FROM THE PUBLISHER ❧

It is unusual for a publisher to insert a page in one of their author's books. However, this is a very unique book and the usual simply doesn't apply. Jane M. Martin's, *Breathe Better, Live in Wellness,* is the flagship book chosen to launch our newly created "Authors Who Make A Difference" program. Jane's book has established the benchmark for future Infinity Publishing titles accepted as part of this dynamic publishing program that will include meaningful books with a high potential to help to significantly improve the quality of life for a vast segment of the population. We believe that over 65 million people suffering with some form of Chronic Lung Disease in the United States constitutes a significant segment of the populace.

Jane contacted us expressing her sincere desire to do a second edition of her highly acclaimed book. She wished to include additional current information, expand her book with more material about pulmonary problems, and share even more encouraging reflections from folks with chronic lung problems who have achieved a higher level of wellness while coping with this disease. We were impressed not only with Jane's passionate desire to make a really good book even better, but to truly see it become a book that would make a difference—giving hope to the many folks living with a Chronic Lung Disease.

There were areas in which she needed her publisher's help; and it was through the efforts of John F. Harnish, our Special Projects Director and Author's Advocate, working closely with Jane that the "Authors Who Make A Difference" program was born.

We, the Infinity Publishing family, thank you for allowing us the privilege of providing this special book for you, and we genuinely hope it will make a positive difference in helping you improve the quality of your life.

Sincerely,

Tom Gregory

President
Infinity Publishing

Table of Contents

Section Five
Interstitial Lung Disease / Pulmonary Fibrosis
Memory Treasures to Store

Section Six
Things That Make It Worse

Relationships: Voices of the Caregiver / Well Spouse

Section Seven
Things That Help
Exercise? Are You Kidding? Pulmonary Rehabilitation

Acknowledgments

I most gratefully acknowledge the generosity of the following people who contributed their stories: Leslie & Linda Blevins, Patrick Dooley, Bill Horden, Marion Hyde, Justin Johnson, Leola Johnson, Harold Lake, Eleanor Lake, Jennifer Lane, Marilou Parker, Mary Pierce, Todd Pierce, Justine Reiger, Joan Savilla, Dave St. Cyr, Shirley St. Cyr, Jo-Von Tucker, Janet Van Dommelen, Jeanette Van Kley, Dale Van Langevelde, Mary Van Langevelde, Julius Ver Hoef, Sammie Wade, Fred Walsh, John Walsh, John Widmayer, Blanche Wilkinson, and Nick Wilkinson.

I thank those who so openly shared their thoughts and experiences in the battle to quit smoking: Jane Gillette, Arlene Rothenberg, and Linda in Pittsburgh.

My sincere appreciation goes to those who offered up their words of wisdom, brief in nature, but brought forth from a long time of trial: Clarence E. Ashley, Betty Biondi, Edwin Brubaker, Nina Caiozzo, Lois Felinski, Chester Flis, Leo F. Hobbs, John Kennedy, Betty Roemer, Stella Surko, and those who wished to remain anonymous.

To Jackie Glass and Sheila Shiel for their honest and inspiring poetry, my deep gratitude to them for having the courage and insight to put their feelings into verse. To John Smith for his gentle heart and his expression of Thanksgiving. To Betty Dotson-Lewis, for her help, and for recognizing the power of stories.

Many thanks to Darlene Watkins for understanding the importance of this project and sharing with me the opportunity of getting to know the dear people of her Pulmonary Rehab program.

My profound appreciation goes to Dr. Rick Carter for proofreading the manuscript and encouraging this endeavor, and to Dr. Steven Kraker for contributing his expertise on oxygen use, his advice, and support.

To Mary Burns for so graciously providing the Forward, and for being a constant source of inspiration to me in my daily work. Thank you so very much.

A heartfelt thank you to Carla Vissers for being my friendly reader so early on and to Catherine Gray for editing as well as for her very helpful suggestions. Thanks also to Erin Scholten and Anthony Fox, first edition word processing wizards.

To my friends Jane Gillette, Mary Pierce, Janet Van-Dommelen, and Jo-Von Tucker, who assured me of the necessity and validity of this project. Their friendship and encouragement have sustained me through this process.

To John F. Harnish at Infinity Publishing for his able assistance, his cheerful encouragement, and warm friendship.

To Cat Wong and Chris Master for their creative gifts in cover design.

To Diane Walsh for just being there.

To Mom and Dad who taught me and showed me that it was right to help people whenever I thought I could.

To my dearest husband Marvin, my best friend and steadfast support. And to our children Corinne and Harrison, who were so patient as I spent many hours in the research and writing of this book.

Finally, to the Pulmonary Rehabilitation Patients at Holland Community Hospital and the members of the Better Breathers' Club of Holland, thank you. You are my teachers. You are my inspiration.

Why This Book?

In my work in Pulmonary Rehabilitation and our local Better Breathers' Club I have usually been able to find suitable educational materials concerning the facts and figures of Chronic Lung Disease. However, when attempting to address the emotional needs of patients who are feeling depressed, isolated, confused, and generally "down in the dumps," I have found very little. Listening to the voices of these patients and hearing their needs, I've felt, at times, so helpless. So, what to do? How could I, a person with healthy lungs—how could I help?

The answer was already there, right in front of me, in my work, in the hearts and minds of the patients themselves. The help was not in me, but within the people I've felt privileged to know—my pulmonary patients. They are the folks who have inspired *me* by the way they have overcome the limitations imposed by their disease, and found a way to live content and joyful lives. The courage and humor possessed by some of my patients, their willingness to learn new things, press on, and live life to the fullest propelled me to work toward a solution. And that solution was to take experiences of those people who had found a positive way to accept their disease, to cope and thrive, and *connect* that to those living in sadness, denial, and confusion. Through listening to the voices of the joyful, and recording the wisdom coming from within them, the connection has been made—and it is here.

As well as being inspired by their wherewithal, I have also found that by living with the daily challenge of breathing well, many of our friends with Chronic Lung Disease have been given—*and seized*—the opportunity to develop great strength of character and perseverance. And through these struggles they have found much richness in life, learning not to take pure, simple pleasures for granted. Many folks with Chronic Lung Disease have learned, also, to have a high level of empathy and caring. So they, in many ways, are best able to help others who are challenged by shortness of breath. Moreover, from these special people, our friends with Chronic Lung Disease, there is much we can *all* learn.

Dear reader, know that for every person who finds help by walking through the door of a Pulmonary Rehabilitation Program or a meeting of a Better Breathers' Club, there are so many more out there who are suffering in silence and isolation, feeling breathless, lonely and uninspired. This book is for them. It is for those who have not had the privilege of knowing people who have met and conquered the challenge of Chronic Lung Disease. It is for those who will never meet the people who have contributed their stories here. It is also for those who participate in Pulmonary Rehabilitation and Better Breathers' Support Groups and wish to learn more about others like themselves. It is for friends and family members of people with Chronic Lung Disease so they may know that there are many other people with the same concerns. It is for those who want to know and need to know that things *can* get better.

How to use this book. Here are the stories of people with Chronic Lung Disease. **Their direct quotes and own words are found in this type.** *The words of the author as introduction to each story and sometimes as part of an interview are in italics.* Each major breathing disorder discussed in this book has its own section. However, by the very nature of Chronic Lung Disease and its varied components, there are people with a mix of several disorders. Consequently there may be valuable information found, for example, on asthma in the COPD section, or on caregiving within a story on COPD or pulmonary fibrosis. It is suggested that you read the entire book, even if not in the order it is printed, so that you may harvest as much information and support as possible.

As part of the research of this book people with Chronic Lung Disease were asked, "If you could say one thing to someone with breathing problems who was about to give up, what would you say?" Their answers can be found throughout the book. Some are echoed in that person's story, but it can be said that wise words sometimes bear repeating. Where there is no name following a quote, it is because that contributor wished to remain anonymous.

When living with a chronic disease and facing their own mortality, many people experience an increased sense of spirituality. This is not necessarily a matter of becoming "religious." But by facing adversity, people often learn to look at self, others, and the world in a fresh way and in a different light. Often this involves discovering a new sense of thankfulness for each day and finding fulfillment in simple joys. The religious expressions found here vary and, in the true spirit of patients helping patients, are in the voice of the contributors. This book espouses no particular religious belief, but was written with respect for the personal spirituality of every human being and the infinite value of inner peace.

Keep in mind that in this book are expressed the personal *opinions and experiences* of people who have met the challenge of living with Chronic Lung Disease. This is not intended as a substitute for medical advice.

Breathe Better, Live in Wellness: Winning Your Battle Over Shortness of Breath. Winning the battle? Does this imply that it is possible to overcome Chronic Lung Disease? To eliminate it from your life? In some cases, there is great potential to control lung disease so symptoms are rare or non-existent. But in many situations, although not possible to get rid of your lung disease, there remains promise of rising above the devastation of shortness of breath into renewed wellness you may have thought was all but lost.

Breathe Better, Live in Wellness will show you how to find current information and resources to improve your breathing. There are resources and information specific to each disease within each chapter. There is a comprehensive list of resources at the end of the book as well. This book will also introduce you to avenues of education and support. But perhaps most importantly, it will grace you with a connection to the inspiring stories shared by others. It is my hope that when you read this book you will feel as if you are sitting down with a dear friend, hearing his or her story. Look in these pages for something near to your heart or that of someone you know. I trust you'll find something familiar, helpful, and inspiring, giving you a renewed sense of under-standing for yourself or your loved one. You are not alone. There is hope for a life with better breathing, renewed wellness, and making a positive difference in the lives of others.

How... This Book?

When I started putting together the first edition of this book, Inspirations: Stories of Breathing Better and Living Well years ago, sending out in the mail those very first questionnaires, I had no idea what to expect. My experience in working with people with Chronic Lung Disease told me they seemed compelled to tell their stories and felt comforted when they found others had similar experiences. The project seemed worthwhile. Still, I wasn't sure how people would react to being asked personal questions about their life with this illness. I expected some doors to be closed in my face. In collecting the material and writing this book, I found very little of that. People have been very willing, even pleased, and they say, "honored," to give of their time—and more importantly—to share their stories, words, and poems, telling of their personal struggles and victories in living with Chronic Lung Disease.

For the most part, in interviewing people, I felt an over-whelming sense of welcome. For some visits I arrived at a home and was greeted with a hug, a meal, coffee or tea. I was treated to a short piano recital, shown craft or garden projects, keepsakes, and pictures of the children and grand-children. These folks talked and talked, their stories unfolding before me. I listened and listened, as they told their stories so eagerly. It is such priceless treasure to hear the story of one's life, no matter what the story is, but more so because of the triumph over this disease, and its promise to help others live better lives.

The lives of people who live each day with Chronic Lung Disease matter. They so very much matter! If their stories are not told, their voices not heard, how will anybody know? How will the people who fear they cannot go on—cannot live with shortness of breath—how will they do it—how will they know? If the stories are not preserved in some way, they will be gone except, perhaps, for some vague verbal accounts passed along to close friends or family, but lost forever to those beyond the circle, those who need them most.

To those people who shared their stories, their experiences, their thoughts and words, a profound **thank you**. Through sharing your stories, please be assured, you have given comfort, support, and hope to people you will never meet. Thank you for your openness, your honesty, and your generosity of spirit. To the loved ones of those who have since passed on, my heartfelt thank you. Please know that your courage as well as the courage and spirit of your beloved lives on in these pages.

To live with Chronic Lung Disease and remain hopeful, content, and in service to others... that is the task. The people whose stories and words are here have accepted it, embraced it, and accomplished it. Job well done.

Foreword

To paraphrase what Dr. Tom Petty writes in *"Enjoying Life with Chronic Obstructive Pulmonary Disease,"* disease is an impairment of an organ system, of its structure, or of its function. An *illness* is the total *impact* of that impairment on the life of the person. Illness deals with the failure to adapt to an impairment, and how this failure to adapt then interferes with daily living. Therefore, a person can have significant disease without having significant illness.

COPD most certainly is a serious disease that can profoundly impact the quality of life. The quotes, vignettes and stories in this book demonstrate how this group of patients has met the challenge of coping with their anxiety, their depression, their shortness of breath, and their limited activities. They have risen above their disease and courageously controlled the amount of illness in their lives.

Their words of wisdom will be an inspiration to everyone reading this book, not just those suffering with respiratory disease. The overall message shining forth from *"Breathe Better, Live in Wellness,"* is that there *is* life after the diagnosis of COPD. And it can be a good life. "You pick yourself up, get help and life goes on" is the philosophy expressed by many of these pulmonary patients. Good advice for all of us!

In reading this book I was touched, awed and inspired by the courage of these patients, as well as the many others I have had the privilege of knowing over the years. I have often asked myself, "Would I have this much strength?" Health care professionals fortunate enough to work in the field of pulmonary rehabilitation become passionate about their profession. Despite the never ending Medicare forms, HMO hassles, and short staffing, our lives are enriched by the constant inspiration we receive from our wonderful patients. I congratulate Jane Martin on her labor of love in gathering the thoughts, advice and philosophies of her patients, families and caregivers in this book, well named *"Breathe Better, Live in Wellness."*

Mary Burns, R.N., B.S.
Executive Vice President,
Pulmonary Education and Research Foundation
Lomita, California

Section One

What Do You Mean I Have a
Chronic Lung Disease?

Don't give up. There is help out there.
--Chester Flis, Detroit, MI

"You have COPD," the doctor said. Joe, a handsome man in his late 60's, heard it and paused. His thoughts were suspended for a moment, a moment that seemed like an hour. Normally a friendly guy, a talker, Joe was now speechless. Anxiety and a thousand questions rose from within, causing him to be breathless—even more so than usual.

His doctor continued, explaining what type of disorder it was and what could be done about it. Maybe Joe heard that. Maybe he didn't.

"You're going to have this for the rest of your life. It's not going to go away."

"I'm always going to be short of breath like this? This is terrible! I can't do anything around the house anymore without gasping."

"Right now you're recovering from a bad bout of pneumonia. We'll do some tests and see how the next few weeks go."

"Now hold on here, doc. The pneumonia came out of the blue. I was fine before that. So pretty soon I should be fine again, right?"

"Well, chances are, this has been coming on for a long time. It can take years before we notice shortness of breath in COPD. Our lungs can put up with quite a bit of abuse."

Only slightly calmer now, Joe said, "OK, doc. So I have this, this COPD, or whatever you want to call it. There must be something that will help. A pill I can take, or something?"

"There are medicines you can take, but this is, for all intents and purposes, irreversible. The damage is done." The doctor repeated, "You'll have this for the rest of your life."

"The rest of my life? Now wait a minute. That sounds so... final. There must be some mistake. I've worked hard all my life. I just retired, and now I've got things to do. Plans to travel. Grandchildren to spoil."

"I know, Joe. I'm sorry. But this is the way it is. The nurse will be back in a few minutes to tell you about your new medicines. I'll see you in a few weeks."

This scene may be familiar to you. But even if it is not, chances are you know someone with whom it is. COPD,

Joe's diagnosis, just one of the disorders covered in this book, is the fourth leading cause of death in the United States (behind heart disease, cancer and stroke), and the only one of the top ten on the rise. COPD deaths in women tripled in the last two decades. It is estimated that as many as 24 million Americans have symptoms of COPD. Despite its ease of diagnosis, COPD remains profoundly under-diagnosed while in its milder and more treatable form.

Following is a very basic explanation of Chronic Lung Disease, the two main categories, *obstructive* and *restrictive*, and some of the disorders within them. In this book CLD is an abbreviation for Chronic Lung Disease, encompassing all the Chronic Lung Diseases, both *obstructive* (emphysema, chronic bronchitis, asthma, Alpha-1 Antitrypsin deficiency, bronchiectasis, and others) and *restrictive* (interstitial lung disease, pulmonary fibrosis, silicosis, sarcoidosis, sclerodema, and many others). CLD in this book covers COPD, COLD and other chronic pulmonary diseases.

COPD stands for "Chronic Obstructive Pulmonary Disease." COLD stands for "Chronic Obstructive Lung Disease." These two terms can be used interchangeably, but may be used exclusively in one geographic region or another. *Chronic* means that the disease is present at all times. It does not go away. *Obstructive* refers to difficulty getting air "out" of the lungs. *Pulmonary*, of course, refers to the lungs. A person with COPD has at least two of the following: emphysema, asthma or chronic bronchitis.

How can someone who does not have lung disease possibly imagine what it is like to work so hard to breathe? This may give you a hint of what it is like. If you do not have lung disease and are in good health, try the following.

Take a big, deep breath. Blow out just part of it. Now try to take another deep breath. You probably feel as if your lungs are over inflated. Do this once again. After several years of breathing this way, the lungs actually get bigger and lose their elastic recoil, which is what originally aided them in expelling stale air. The more damaged portion of the lungs compress the better parts like an inflated automobile air bag. The lungs don't have much room to move. The air sacs where oxygen exchange takes place, as well as the tubes that connect the air sacs to your trachea, or windpipe, become damaged and weak and can collapse. This is **emphysema.** Its main cause is cigarette smoking and exposure to air pollution. There is difficulty in getting air **out** of the lungs making emphysema an **obstructive** lung disease. Emphysema is chronic in nature because it has evolved over a long time and even on good days, it is always there.

Another form of emphysema is **Alpha-1 Antitrypsin Deficiency, (A-1AD)**, which is inherited. This disease strikes people in their 20's, 30's, 40's, and 50's. People who have inherited an altered AAT gene from each parent are considered to have severe deficiency and likely to develop the disease.

Now pinch your nose so you can breathe only through your mouth. Breathe out through a straw. Pinch the straw until it is almost closed off. In **asthma** the bronchial tubes, or airways, inside the lungs are inflamed or swollen and then squeezed and tightened by constricting muscles in the airways. Thick mucous clogging the bronchial tubes also restricts the ability to breathe. There is difficulty in getting air out of the lungs. **Asthma** is an **obstructive** disease but although *not curable,* is considered *controllable and reversible.*

Chronic Bronchitis is when the lining of the airways becomes inflamed and irritated by long term exposure to tobacco smoke and / or pollution. With chronic bronchitis there is a lot of thick mucous production, causing a cough on most mornings. In this disease the lungs' natural cleaning system, cilia, millions of tiny hair-like structures that normally sweep mucous upward, become destroyed or paralyzed. **Chronic Bronchitis** is another **obstructive** lung disorder.

4

Having a **Restrictive Lung Disease** means there is trouble getting air **into** the lungs and / or trouble getting oxygen into the bloodstream. **Pulmonary Fibrosis** is when the lung tissue is stiff or scarred. There is trouble getting oxygen from the air into the alveoli (air sacs at the ends of the airways) and then into the blood. **Idiopathic (cause unknown) pulmonary fibrosis,** is one of many disorders in a large category called **interstitial lung disease**. Just a few of the 130 disorders in this category include asbestosis, coal worker's pneumoconiosis (Black Lung Disease), sarcoidosis, silicosis, and Wegener's Granulomatosis.

It is also important to note that many patients may have more than one of these processes going on in their lungs. A person may have components of both Obstructive and Restrictive Lung Disease.

Now you have an idea of what goes on in the lungs with some pulmonary disorders. What is it like to live day after day with shortness of breath?

Try this: Go to your favorite chair. Sit there until you absolutely need to get up to go to the kitchen or the bathroom. Get up from the chair, stay right there, and breathe very shallowly at a rate of about 24 breaths per minute. Breathing this way, walk to your destination. Stay there for 20 minutes. You can now go back to your chair. Try this also with a 50-foot hose connected to your face. This may give you some idea of the daily existence for many people with Chronic Lung Disease.

Can you imagine trying to get out to perform necessary tasks such as doing the weekly shopping for groceries or getting medicine when you have this much trouble just getting around the house? How about playing with the grandchildren or simply taking a walk? Is it any wonder that some people with Chronic Lung Disease become depressed and difficult to be around?

But there really is help and hope! Please read on and learn what you or your loved ones, in spite of shortness of breath, can do to *breathe better and live in wellness!*

Section Two

COPD

Chronic Obstructive Pulmonary Disease

Never give up. There is much worse. Life is precious.

--Betty Biondi, Detroit, MI

Think Positive and Help Yourself

Justine

*"There are too many things to see and learn about,
too many things that I want to see."*
Clarence E. Ashley, Rochester, MI

*It took me over two years to finally meet Justine Reiger
after first learning of her battle with emphysema. In search
of words of wisdom and inspiration from lung patients, I had
sent questionnaires to a Pulmonary Rehab program director
in the Detroit area with whom I was acquainted. Darlene,
the director, distributed the questionnaires to people in her
program and returned the completed ones to me. When I
opened the packet I found remarkable stories and words of
encouragement from pulmonary patients to pulmonary
patients. Within Justine's response I read the words of a
spirited lady whom I hoped that someday I would have the
honor of meeting.*

*I drove to Detroit excitedly, but a bit nervous. I would
be spending the day interviewing somebody whom I'd never
met. As I walked up the driveway to the house Justine
greeted me, holding the front door open as I entered her
home. The first thing I noticed about Justine was her friend-*

8

liness. The next thing I noticed was her size. She is a petite lady, standing about 4 feet, 11 inches tall. She wore a yellow polo shirt, blue jeans and white sneakers. In spite of her size she exuded an energy and a fiery tenacity that I already knew had served her well. I immediately felt at ease. She had prepared us a light lunch. We sat down to eat and began to talk. Justine was direct, at times blunt, but always enthusiastic and with a wonderful sense of humor.

Growing up just outside the City of Detroit in the mid 50's, Justine Reiger considered herself poor but happy. She lived in the middle of Grosse Pointe, an extremely affluent suburb populated by automotive company executives and their families. Being in the midst of enormous wealth, but not directly a part of it, was her family's way of life.

What was your life like growing up in that city at that time?

"The maids, the chauffeurs, and the gardeners, people who worked on these estates, had to have a place to live. So there were two blocks in Grosse Pointe that all the help lived on. My father worked as a gardener for the Dodge estate for years. The Dodges had a beautiful home on the lake—a mansion. They had a big Yacht called the Delphine. My father was also the first mate on the boat."

The members of Justine's family were no strangers to serving the Grosse Pointe elite. A sense of pride came through as Justine explained that her grandfather had worked for the Dodge family on their farm. Her uncle was a chauffeur and handyman. Justine's mother supplemented the family income by taking in laundry and ironing for some of Grosse Pointe's upper class. Justine and her big brother, the only other child in her immediate family, had a good life. They were part of a loving family and were deeply religious.

They attended the local Catholic school with the wealthy children.

"In the Catholic School everybody was considered equal. Everybody wore uniforms. Everybody was treated the same.

"But *of course* I couldn't help but notice that the other girls were rich. They drove their own cars. I walked. They lived in beautiful big homes—estates. I had a very nice comfortable home but it was not set up for entertaining. When I was invited to their parties I was ecstatic! After a while I started going to a lot of different parties. One day I was invited to join their group, the most popular girls' club at school. All the girls smoked. Now remember, this was in an era when 'everybody' smoked; movie stars, models, even our own doctor! So I started smoking. It was cool. It was the thing to do. It just seemed to make me feel grown up, accepted."

Justine's father, a heavy smoker of Camels, advised her.

"He didn't want me to start. Not because it was unhealthy, but because it was expensive and it was just a dirty habit."

It was the 1950's. Times were good. The automotive industry was booming. Teens were not the least bit concerned about what smoking might do to their health.

"Nobody knew then that it was so bad for us. We were just out having fun."

So Justine, the daughter of the hired help became one of the girls. Today she laughs as she says, "Maybe I would have been better off if I hadn't!"

Following high school Justine went to work as a secretary, got married, and had three children. Her life took a sad turn when her dear brother was diagnosed with leukemia. After a valiant fight with the disease he died at age 54. Justine was devastated. Less than three months later her mother-in-law passed away, leaving Justine and other family members to care for her father-in-law who was in a nursing home, comatose, for the last three years of his life.

"We took turns visiting him. In case he woke up we wanted him to recognize somebody there. So much happened to our family within such a short time. I never really seemed to recover from one loss when we were hit with another one."

Not too long before these hard times, back when Justine was 45 years old, she had noticed a little shortness of breath but hadn't paid any attention to it. One night, at age 50, however, she had a big scare.

"I woke up in the middle of the night and I couldn't breathe. I just sat up in bed and *I could not breathe*! It was terrible. I didn't know what to think. I thought I was going to die! I was absolutely petrified.

"My doctor thought it was an asthma attack and after I recovered from that episode they were treating it as that. Then I got a big infection and was in the hospital for three weeks, one week in intensive care. That's when they started calling it COPD. I was devastated—scared!

"The first thing I did was I stopped smoking. It was the hardest thing I ever tried to do, but I knew it had to be done. I prayed and chewed Nicorette gum until I lost my fillings! After that near deadly stay in the hospital I never smoked again. It was so good to be free!

"As far as the diagnosis of COPD was concerned, of course I had a few questions. I knew I had to learn a lot because I was going to manage somewhat my own health care along with my doctor. I was going to be responsible for changes in my life and how I handled all this. I went to the library to see what I could find about COPD. I found very, very, very little, and what I did find was outdated. As I began learning about COPD, it was a real low point—a shock—when I realized there was *no cure*! It is hard to accept that there is nothing you or anyone can do to reverse the damage to your lungs. Something I did find, though, said that after diagnosis, a person has 5-10 years to live.

"I thought, '*My goodness, I've already had this as far as we could figure, maybe two…three years. You know, I was a young person!   I've only got…seven…eight… years left?   I'm not going to see grandchildren?*

"Now I look back on that. So much has happened in my life in the last 10 years. To think that I would have missed all that! Yes, when I read this I felt terrified—and very depressed.

>➤ I Wanted to Live! ➤<

"But, see, that is what the *book* had said. My doctor never said that. He was always very optimistic. After reading about this life expectancy I asked my doctor at one visit if he thought it was a good idea for me to make any long range investment plans. He just laughed."

So what turned this around for you? What helped you to go on and fight?

"My husband always had a positive attitude with me, encouraging me. My doctor and husband were always upbeat and encouraging, giving me a measure of hope. I thought very highly of my doctor. He had sat with me in intensive care for 24 hours. In fact, at the Catholic Hospital, the sister thought he was my husband!

"I also started thinking of my brother and his battle with leukemia, and how they had given him just a short time to live. That boy fought until he took his very last breath. *He taught me courage. He never gave up hope.*

"I thought, 'Well, I'm the only one left. My brother's gone, my mother too, my dad, my grandparents.... You know, I'm pretty lucky. I'm still here and I've got a lot to look forward to. I'm not going to disappoint my family by being a horse's ass and sitting here all depressed and feeling sorry for myself! I'll just try my best and hope as my family in heaven looks down they will see that I am trying too – to fight a good fight. *I'm going to do something about this!* I'm going to do whatever I can. Even if it takes a little therapy, I'll see a psychologist. I'll go and do whatever I can.'

"I decided I would do what I could to stay as well as I could for as long as I could. I decided I'd also pray for a miracle and healing.

"My doctor, an allergist / internist strongly recommended Pulmonary Rehab. Remember, I thought very highly of my doctor. You know, he had stood by me and encouraged me all the way. He told me, 'You're a very young person. You have to do what you can to help yourself.'"

So what was it like for you at Rehab? How did you feel about that? Tell me about your first day.

"You know, I'm kind of self-conscious. I was a little leery about going to Rehab and meeting everybody. I didn't know *what* to expect. I didn't know if there were going to be people in gym clothes. I mean, when you see people exercise on television... they're in their little thongs!

"On my first day of Rehab I was scared. I thought, *Oh boy*. I looked at all the equipment and everything. I saw the Cardiac Rehab class finishing up, and they go *fast*. I didn't think I'd be able to do it.

"But the girls on the rehab staff were *so* nice. Darlene said, 'Don't worry, you won't be in *that* group!' They [the staff] couldn't have been any nicer. They'd say, 'We're going to try this and if you're not comfortable, you just tell us and we'll stop.'

"Now I go three days a week and it helps me a lot. It's a good excuse to get out of the house, meet new people and sometimes I get the opportunity to help someone just coming into the program.

"One new person coming into the program, an older gentleman, said on his first day, 'I can't do this. They're gonna kill me!'

"I said, 'No they won't. They'll take it very easy and you'll be fine.' Now he's off oxygen and on maintenance [a continuing exercise program following completion of the basic course of treatment]. He is really neat. He has a wonderful sense of humor. I could see a change from an insecure, 'Gee, I can't do this. It would be so much easier to get it over with, to die,' to 'I feel better and I'm not as bad as I thought I was.'

"Pulmonary Rehab changes lives, it really does."

Justine, why do you think that some people do as you have done, taking charge of their health, staying positive, and others do not?

Without a second of hesitation she says, "It's got to be in your upbringing and education.

"I was taught in school that with the help of God you can do *anything*. No matter how bad things are, it *can* turn around. All you have to do is reach out. It's only a prayer away. Now that's the way we were raised.

"I lost the sight in my right eye when I was two years old. It didn't bother me so much because I was too young to realize it. As I got older, though, I thought about my mother, what she went through, having to see her little girl lose an eye. She coped with all that. She didn't sit around feeling sorry for herself. She never felt sorry for me. She never treated me any different. The same thing was true for school. No one was *allowed* to tease me. There were *no* eye jokes and *no* short jokes.

"Our parents lived through depression, they lived through World Wars. You just don't give up. Life goes on and, you know, under the most horrible circumstances, you go on and you survive. That's just the way I was taught.

"Our whole family has been raised to help one another. My dad was ill for many years. I lost a brother to cancer. We took care of my grandmother who lived to be 99. We just take care of each other. For me, I have been overwhelmed by my family's love and support.

"Now I thank God everyday for what health I have and for guidance in selecting the right doctors and treatments. As far as the COPD is concerned, people with this disease must know that there are things they can do to help themselves. But that's not enough—they've got to *do* it! They've got to learn as much as they can and then comply with it.

>*** Find Good Advice, Take It, and Use It ! ***<

What would you say to someone who might notice some mild to moderate shortness of breath and / or some decrease in their ability to do things—in order to spark their interest in starting to seek information?

"I don't think I'd be as bad as I am if the doctor, an obstetrician, would have followed up on something. When I had my son Christopher who is now 33, the doctor said, 'Hmmmm...You're wheezing a little bit.'

"At the time I didn't think anything of it. I didn't know I was wheezing. I didn't know what wheezing was.

"The doctor asked, 'Are you still smoking?'

"I told him I was. And he never said anything else. Maybe if he would have said, 'You know, you should quit smoking, you should see your medical doctor...' if he had pushed a little harder on me at that point... But he didn't say *anything*. I never thought of it again because he made so light of it.

"And then later he said, 'It sounds like asthma.'

"I'm wondering if I had this a long time and nobody ever picked up on it. I'm not blaming this on anybody else. I mean, I did it. But nobody told me about smoking being related to lung disease. I mean, at the time, we didn't know it."

How do you reconcile that you did this to yourself?

"Well, I feel terrible! I did it myself, but it wasn't all my fault. I feel that the tobacco companies deceived the public terribly. By the time the warnings began to come out, it was too late for me. I was hooked.

"I'm just so glad that we're all aware of what's going on now. It's too late for me to benefit from this information. I'm glad that so far none of my grandchildren smoke. I am very vocal when given the opportunity and work for a smoke free environment in any public place.

"My advice is: If you smoke, quit. Find out everything you can about COPD and make sure you've got a good specialist with good current information. And then—do what you're told!"

You were fortunate enough to have Lung Volume Reduction Surgery[1] with an unusually great outcome, but even before that you made up your mind to be very pro-active in your care and management of this disease. What would you suggest to others who might be suspecting they have a serious breathing problem and are afraid of seeking help or just don't know where to turn?

1.) "Make sure what you're reading is up-to-date and current.

2.) "Make sure you have a physician who is current on what is going on with the disease that you have, regardless of what it is. I mean, if you've got cancer, you're not going to go to a podiatrist! You're going to find someone in that field with wonderful credentials, and you're going to go to that person. You're not going to go to someone around the corner because they're close to your house.

Some people don't want to leave their long time physician who is not providing proper care and treatment. They are sometimes fond of their doctor and would feel badly leaving him or her. What would you say to them?

"That doctor is not doing right by you and you're not doing right by yourself. You can still go to your old family doctor, but for your lungs, go to somebody else. When it comes to a major disease, you go to a specialist. If you don't know anybody call and check with a university or the American Lung Association and get a recommendation.

"Under the guidance of your doctor manage your own care. My doctor was very interested in what was happening and he kept current on everything. And when there was no more that he could do, he sent me to the University of Michigan.

What about Pulmonary Rehab? Many people don't go because they don't see how exercise and education can possibly help them.

"I think that if the doctors were more emphatic about it... if they said, 'I *want* you to do this. You *have* to do this. I won't take care of you if you don't cooperate,' I think that more people would go. Definitely. Get involved in Pulmonary Rehab.

"I have met several people that have been told they have COPD and know nothing about inhalers or nebulizers or the different drugs available to help because they have doctors that don't inform them or tell them *where* to go for information. The importance of using inhalers and medications properly, and following directions, must be stressed. These are things that are learned in Pulmonary Rehabilitation."

What is your life like today? Do you feel that you have limitations?

"I get short of breath if I do a whole lot of walking, you know, if I do a whole lot of shopping. If I get short of breath though, now, I sit down and I've got my breath back in a matter of seconds. Before, I couldn't get it back. I could sit and huff and puff for an hour and I'd use my inhalers and everything else.

"I still get short of breath, but I get through all my exercises. I don't have to stop. I do a lot. I go to the grocery store, the mall, play cards with my friends, and I go out to lunch with the girls. My family is absolutely thrilled."

What is the most important thing you've learned?

"Everybody's got to find their own solution. I can only tell them what's helped me. I would say, 'Stop feeling sorry for yourself and find out what you can do to help yourself. There are many things that you can do to help. Take your medications, follow a good diet, *exercise* and work for a smoke free environment. Take good advice and use it. And pray, pray, and pray some more!'"

Justine Reiger

COPD Facts

- COPD is the fourth leading cause of death in the United States and the only one of the ten top causes that is on the rise.

- 10% of the population aged 65 years and older is estimated to have COPD.

- Approximately 24 million Americans have evidence of impaired lung function consistent with a diagnosis of COPD.

From the US COPD Coalition Website.
www.uscopd.com

People suffering from lung diseases often do not receive proper treatment because they do not know what they are suffering from, or how serious it is. The first international survey of COPD showed that 20% of people with the illness could not name it and 46% continued to smoke, even though smoking is the main cause of their disease. 64% of patients were being treated by their general practitioner and only 20% had been examined by a respiratory specialist.

Reuters, October 2, 2002. www.reuters.com

Do Something to Help Someone

Jeanette

"There is always a way to make a contribution."
Mary Pierce, St. Joseph, MI

When thinking of spirited people I knew personally with Chronic Lung Disease, my thoughts didn't have to go far. This is the story of my eldest aunt who inspired not only our family, but so many others with her spunky spirit, powerful song, and "never-say-die" attitude.

Long before it was common to hear of cultural diversity, my Aunt Jenny routinely opened her home to people from many different lands. My most vivid memories of my aunt are of her, her daughter, and my mother serving Sunday dinners at her home. This meal was always crowded, the table so loaded that a tea cart next to my aunt's chair held more food. As a child, squeezed between my father and my sister, I'd sit at that table across from my Native American cousin, her husband of Dutch decent, and their children. Between bites of potato and roast beef, I'd learn something from our guest about life in Sweden, Arabia, India, or some other far away place. But more importantly, I learned that people are people, no matter where they come from. At the close of

21

each meal our guest would offer a prayer in his or her native tongue. The rest of us didn't understand the words, but we knew that God did, and that just made everything feel all right.

Aunt Jenny was a wiry, brusque, no-nonsense woman who lived by her parents' teachings: **"Work hard and share what you have."**

Sadly, my Aunt Jeanette passed away before the work on this book was complete. She died quietly, alone in her apartment, and true to form, it was only hours after doing some work on a project for her church.

Jeanette Van Kley grew up on her family's small farm in South Holland, Illinois, 20 miles south of downtown Chicago. The eldest of three children, she spent much of her time at home working in the onion and tomato fields.

"I had to wear those big bib overalls then and they were hot! I don't ever want to wear them again. My sister and brother and I spent many hours pulling tomato worms off each plant. We placed them in a bag and then burned them. Those were the days before pesticides. There was no irrigation and every evening we'd go out with a bucket of water and a dipper to give each plant a drink."

When not doing chores or attending school, Jeanette taught herself to read music at home by practicing the organ and playing from the only written music in the family home, an old hymnbook. In the days when most young women in that town didn't think of going on to attain education beyond the eighth grade let alone high school, Jeanette attended college on a scholarship and majored in pre-law. In addition to this demanding schedule she found time to pursue vocal training at the American Conservatory of Music in Chicago. Following college she worked as a secretary / legal assistant in small smoked-filled insurance and law offices for just short of 50 years. She never smoked cigarettes herself.

After getting married Jeanette continued to use her musical and leadership abilities and volunteer spirit by directing music groups at church and teaching Sunday school. She and her husband, Art, also traveled overseas and shared their home throughout the years with many people from around the world including missionaries, foreign exchange students and youths who needed guidance. They became foster parents to a Native American girl whom they eventually adopted.

Jeanette first started to notice difficulty breathing when she contracted tuberculosis in 1974. She had come in contact with the disease in Arabia where she visited a TB hospital with a missionary friend. Ten years later she was diagnosed with emphysema.

In spite of severe emphysema Jeanette lived each day to the fullest. For the last few years of her life, following Art's death, she lived alone in a senior apartment complex, still keeping a small office in her living room. Emotionally, she believed that keeping a positive attitude and keeping busy within limitations helped her to live each day with her lung disease. She directed vocal and bell choirs and volunteered for the local hospital until not long before her death. She found tremendous joy in the company of her family, especially her three grandchildren and four great-grandchildren. Medically, she was always very compliant with taking medications and staying away from things that could have triggered infections. Spiritually, she was inspired by words from the Bible and by prayer. Jeanette felt that patience was the most important thing she learned from life with her illness.

"Some things you cannot do—there are many things you can."

It is not surprising to hear her simple but direct response when asked, "If you could say one thing to somebody with Chronic Lung disease who is about to give up, what would you say?" Jeanette said simply, "Do something to help someone."

She was also quick to add that the following Bible verses that had been so helpful in her battle with lung disease.

"Trust in the Lord with all your heart and lean not unto your own understanding. In all your ways acknowledge him and he will direct your paths."
Proverbs 3:5-6

"In quietness and in confidence shall be your strength.
Isaiah 30:15

Jeanette Van Kley at work in the church office

Harold and Eleanor: A Love Story

Herk

"There is much joy in life, especially if you have grandchildren, children, and a spouse."
Leola Johnson, Holland, MI

When I think of Harold "Herk" and Eleanor Lake, a few words instantly come to mind. Devotion. Commitment. Love. Sure, you might expect a couple in their 60's to have a deep devotion and commitment to each other. But when I saw Herk and Eleanor look at each other or even speak about each other I could tell that they were absolutely in love. When one of them walked into the room the other would just glow. This is the story of Herk and Eleanor Lake and how together they battled Herk's COPD and lung cancer.

Herk Lake walked into the Cardiac/Pulmonary exercise gym, looking dusky blue. We could see, even from a distance, that this man was working hard to breathe. Seated at the main desk at one end of this room, the exercise physiologist and I watched Herk as he walked slowly from the far end of the place, making his way through the maze of exercise bikes, treadmills, and rowing machines. My co-worker, who worked mostly with cardiac patients, noticed Herk's color and quietly said to me, "He's got to be one of yours."

Herk was a rather slight man, maybe 5' 6" tall. He wore aviator eye glasses and a serious look on his face. He handed me a prescription slip with the words, "Pulmonary Rehab" scrawled and signed by his doctor.

"Hello," he said softly. **"My doctor said I should come down here and sign up for this program."**

Herk and I talked for a little while about what had happened with his breathing; his lung cancer which was now gone, and his COPD. We made a date for Herk's initial evaluation for Pulmonary Rehabilitation.

Herk's wife, Eleanor, came with him on that first day and each day thereafter. She looked much younger than her 60 some years. She was a pretty lady with ivory smooth skin and auburn hair in soft, short curls. She had a sweet voice and exuded a deep concern and tenacious love for Herk.

Before becoming better acquainted with the couple at that first meeting, I assumed that theirs was a later-in-life marriage. Surely, I thought, nobody married for more than 20 years looks at their spouse that way. But I was wrong.

Herk started Rehab, having adjusted his part-time job schedule around his exercise class schedule. Herk worked as the hospital courier driving over 100 miles a day. Eleanor always accompanied him.

One day Herk was at Pulmonary Rehab, as part of his usual exercise routine riding the stationary bike. I was going from patient to patient, checking oxygen levels with the pulse oximeter. Herk jerked his head toward the other side of the room, glancing over to Eleanor, who was sitting on a chair near the door, reading a magazine. Half smiling, he said to me, **"Ask her about her long hair."**

"What? Her hair? Did it used to be long?"

"Yeah, ask her about her long hair." He had a look on his face. It was *that* look that only men in their 60's and 70's get when they are out to have some good-natured fun. It was the look of playful misbehavior. The look of the little boy all grown up, half a century later, still chipper and just a bit feisty.

I was somehow sure that he knew exactly what Eleanor's response would be. I had no idea what he was getting at but I was having fun because on this day Herk was up to something, and whatever it was, had nothing to do with concern over catching his next breath.

"That's all I'm going to tell you. Just ask her."

"OK, I'm game."

After completing that round of oximetry checks I went over and asked Eleanor, "Now, what's this about your ...long hair, or something?"

She looked up. "Oh!" With a breathy groan, Eleanor closed the magazine and dropped it to her lap. Exasperated, she tossed a playful scowl toward Herk and said to me, "Did he tell you about *that*?"

"No, not really. He wouldn't say anything else."

"Well, he used to make me so mad! And he knows it."

I looked back at Herk. Yep, they were smiling and laughing and teasing each other—and me. Herk was here among new friends and his beloved Eleanor, exercising and feeling well. I was in the middle of it all and I loved it.

A few years later I visited Eleanor just four days after Christmas. She was, as always, sweet and friendly and with a warm hug graciously welcomed me into her home. We sat next to her beautiful little Christmas tree, among soft twinkling lights and her small collection of miniature lighted houses. It was then that I learned not only of the hair, but the story of Eleanor's life with Herk.

"I was seventeen years old and working at the Warm Friend Hotel as an elevator operator. Herk was working at the telegraph office in the same building. He'd come along and go like this [she slowly and softly stroked her hair from the top of her head down past her shoulders], and stroke my hair like this."

Did you like it when he did that?

"It just drove me up the wall! I wanted nothing to *do* with him! Why, I'd get in the elevator, go up and get it stuck between two floors until the buzzer rang. When he touched my hair like that it really bugged me. You know, he was teasing me.

"Well, one day I was busy doing something else and my mother was working for me in my place.

"When I came back to work she said to me, 'That boy ... Harold... is his name? He came to tell you good-bye.'

"I said... "Good-bye?"

"Yes, he's leaving for the Coast Guard."

Eleanor gasped. "Oh, and I've been so *mean* to him!"

"I felt *so bad*. I asked my mother, 'What can I do?'

"Well, he's going to come back in."

"So when he came back in I told him, 'I'm sorry for the way I've treated you... it wasn't right.'

"And he said, 'That's alright. When I touched your hair like that I was teasing you.'

"So we dated."

28

When Herk, just seventeen years old as well, came home on leave they dated some more. And they fell in love.

One time when Herk was stationed in Charleston, South Carolina, Eleanor went to visit him. One evening during her stay she and Herk were out with friends, another young couple. One of the friends said, "Why don't you guys get married? C'mon. We'll stand up for you."

Herk and Eleanor just looked at each other and decided that was what they'd do. And they did. The teens, now all of 18 years old, had no car in Charleston. And the four friends set out walking, looking for a Justice of the Peace.

"We walked and walked and walked and finally found a Justice of the Peace. It was about nine o'clock and he and his wife were about ready to leave for a party. But they looked at us and said, 'OK, we'll marry you.'

"And we were married."

Eleanor recalls, "After that I went back home and because Herk was in the Coast Guard we lived apart on and off for about a year and four months. Sure, we missed each other terribly, but we knew it wouldn't be too long—and we just got through it."

Following his service in the Coast Guard Herk and Eleanor settled into a home together and had three children.

When he was in his early 60's, Herk first realized there was something wrong with his breathing when he noticed a bad cough. A chest x-ray revealed a tumor in his right lung. Years of insult to his lungs were catching up with him. A family history of lung cancer, smoking cigarettes since age 15, and working in security in the midst of sugar dust at a candy factory eventually added up to very serious problems with his lungs.

Following surgery to remove the cancerous part of his lung, Herk completed Pulmonary Rehab and continued in the Phase III, maintenance, program. As a result of working in the rehab program Herk felt much better and had more stamina. He was even able to do some everyday activities with using less supplemental oxygen. His breathing was easier and more controlled.

Over the next couple years Herk and Eleanor kept in touch with the Rehab staff. In spite of excellent care Herk's ability to remain physically active diminished. He still drove the courier route, but Eleanor now did the running, going in and out of each facility to deliver and receive packages.

One day Eleanor came down to the Pulmonary Rehab department. I knew immediately that something was wrong. I'd never seen that look on her face before. She looked worried, confused, and very anxious. She stood in the doorway so as not to interrupt the class. I went over to her and she broke down, saying, "The cancer's back and they've given Herk six months to live."

After some cancer treatment, Herk and Eleanor returned to their refuge, their summer place, a mobile home in their favorite spot near a lake about 60 miles North of home. Herk spent many hours, day and night, sitting at the kitchen table, short of breath and in pain from the cancer. "He was very uncomfortable. He was not able to lay down in bed."

Many times Eleanor had to get up in the middle of the night to care for him. "He would feel bad asking me to get up again and do something for him, but I'd say, No, that's OK."

"I was so tired. But I just did it. I was glad I could help him. And we found that we had many good friends up there who were so kind to us. They would sit with Herk so I could go out for a little while, or they would bring in delicious meals. That really helped us. And it meant *so* much."

Herk Lake lost his long battle with lung cancer that summer. In sickness and in health, Eleanor was by her husband's side to the very end. As she looks back at her experience with the love of her life, Eleanor knows that the most important thing both she and Herk learned about COPD and cancer was to not take life nor love, *not a single minute of it*, for granted. To this day, Eleanor still misses Herk terribly but takes great comfort in her memories and the life and love they shared.

Could You Have COPD?

- Are you 45 or older, currently smoke cigarettes or have smoked in the past?

- Are you 45 or older and have a history of breathing irritants in your environment?

- Do you sometimes have coughing fits or breathing trouble when exerting?

- Do you have frequent bouts of bronchitis?

- Do you cough up mucus or phlegm in the morning?

- Does asthma, bronchitis, or emphysema run in your family?

If you answered "yes" to any of these questions, you might have COPD. Ask your doctor about taking a simple spirometry (lung function) test. This test takes only a few minutes. Visit www.nlhep.org (The National Lung Health Education Program) for more information.

Herk at rehab

Herk and Eleanor at their place on the lake

Don't Give Up!

Justin

" Be not afraid."
Jeremiah 1:8
Leo F. Hobbs, Roseville, MI

It took only ten minutes to drive from my house in town to the home of Justin and Leola Johnson, but on that day, for some reason, it seemed a world away. I arrived at eleven A.M. to their property that was on that crisp, sunny February morning blanketed in sparkling snow. The little farm seemed to rise from the flat fields that surrounded it, standing serenely steadfast, old and wise on that small patch of God's earth.

As I approached the house, Leola greeted me at the door. Her hair was as white as the snow-covered fields and she wore a pretty denim blouse. A tabby cat slowly stretched at her feet. On the deck at the threshold lay a smooth rock, about six inches round in which the word "hope" was carved.

Inside the house, not far from the door, was an oxygen concentrator. Its quiet, constant hum was background music for our conversation. Justin, who prefers to be called Jud, was at the kitchen table, his hair also white, as was his beard. Always looking the quintessential professor, he sat quietly against a backdrop of large windows. His view was of the long road I'd just driven, on this day looking like a straight ribbon of grey coming through the bright white snow-covered fields. From the windows you could also see a few nearby farms, the Johnson's barn, trees, and most closely a collection of bird feeders.

Jud Johnson grew up in Hamilton, Michigan, the seventh of eight children, the fifth of six boys. His father died of pneumonia when Jud was only six years old. The Johnson children at that time ranged from eighteen to three years of age. Taking care of the chickens, cows, and pigs, picking beans and cucumbers, and pumping water are what Jud remembers about growing up on that farm. He has rather vivid memories as well of his first encounter with smoking.

"See, my older brothers had a small machine that was used to roll tobacco in paper to make cigarettes. They wouldn't let us younger guys use their machine and their tobacco, so my brother Andy, who was two years older, and I, went out and just got some silk off the corn. We rolled it in the paper and smoked it. It was horrible stuff!"

Jud got his first job working in a furniture factory. Following that, he was employed in a boat factory at age nineteen, where as a talented woodworker he specialized in finishing galleys. In those days, asbestos was used as insulation. After working with boats for close to 30 years, Jud went to work cutting metal with abrasive wheels, working with a lot of dust. At the time, he didn't know that all these things

34

were very bad for his lungs. Looking back on it, he is sure these exposures "made things worse."

In August of 1947, Jud and Leola were married. They settled into their own home in the country, only about a block away from where they currently reside. They had four children. Life was good. "We had our own little baseball field in the back. We even had a backstop."

At age 45, Jud, who had always been athletic, noticed he was becoming short of breath when running. His doctor's answer? "Quit running." That response by Jud's physician was definitely inappropriate, although typical of established treatment trends back then. Unfortunately there are still physicians today who give that kind of advice! Knowing what he now knows about the treatment of Chronic Lung Disease, Jud says at that point he should have sought more information about the cause of his shortness of breath and kept on exercising.

Jud knew that something was happening concerning his health, but he didn't know what it was. He did know one thing for sure:

"Things were changing. I missed playing ball with the kids."

Jud worked until retirement at age 63, but didn't stop working altogether, and for a while had a blueberry business. The owner of a cottage on a small inland lake, Jud always enjoyed water skiing. He skied for the last time at age 68, pushing himself to prove that he could do it. He was assured by a nurse friend, who was in the boat at that time, that she would help him if he got into trouble. So away he went. He did it! But in spite of being able to accomplish this, he knew that his limited ability to breathe was really slowing him down. Always an active, athletic man, he now faced an uncertain future.

"Jud liked to make nice things out of wood and had a sense of accomplishment when he could give or sell something he had made," adds Leola.

In spite of having an air cleaner in his shop, the wood dust was causing more and more trouble with his breathing. The steps coming up from his shop were becoming difficult to climb. Giving up woodworking, something he loved, was another loss.

Jud slowly nods and he says, "That was *really* hard."

Loss is experienced by most every person with Chronic Lung Disease. Realization of the inability to physically do things, to move around rather effortlessly as one has in the past, can be most confusing. People often ask themselves, "What is happening here?" In Jud's case he knew somehow that "things were changing." With Chronic Lung Disease, more so than with most other illnesses, changes occur very gradually. These changes can be so insidious that they are usually not even noticed at first, or may be passed off as caused by advancing age or just being "out of shape."

There is almost always one especially defining episode or event that makes a person take notice that there is something very wrong with their breathing. It might be a bout of pneumonia, a failure to keep up with friends or family at a special event, or simply one day unusual difficulty in climbing the stairs. In Jud's case, it was not being able to run with his children. Sooner or later, the wake-up call does come. Then, after a while, when the storm of the wake-up call has passed, there rises a crushing sense of loss, that life as one has known it is gone forever.

The possibility of LVRS (Lung Volume Reduction Surgery) gave Jud some hope for better breathing. This surgery involves removing the upper 30% of the lungs in order to give the remaining portion of the lungs more room to move within the chest. But because Jud's lung damage was too diffuse, or spread throughout all areas of his lungs, he did not qualify. The news that he would not be having the surgery was very disappointing, and a real low point in Jud's battle with Chronic Lung Disease.

"I knew then that there would be no quick fix. That was really hard. I was sort of depressed. Spending time with my wife and my kids, and the grandchildren, enjoying time with them gave me the urge to go on. And time... time and my faith in God helped me get through it. I've learned that health is important but your relationship with God is more important.

"I figure I now have about 20% lung function left. I had 25% about five years ago. Last November we saw the doctor and he said there was really nothing new he could do for me. I started drinking black tea three times a day and I think it helps. I feel much better.

Jud still takes his medications faithfully as directed, uses oxygen 24 hours a day, and exercises by walking one quarter of a mile on his treadmill. Most of all he maintains a strong faith and a positive attitude.

There is silence in the kitchen and Leola slowly reaches to the middle of the table, putting a mug down in front of me. On the mug is a picture of a frog, his head deep in the mouth of a pelican. The frog's front legs reach out from the mouth and have a tight grip around the neck of the bird. The caption is: "Never Give Up!"

Leola says, "See, in the morning I put his cup down... and then... I turn it a little..." Smiling in a bit of a mischievous way, she very slowly turns the mug to make sure Jud sees the picture and the words. Together they smile, then laugh.

"She keeps me going. She'll say, 'You're going to walk today, *aren't you?*' And I say, "Well, I guess so."

"And he does. He's a very determined person. He's got unusual determination."

I remind Jud that he has had this struggle with breathing for over 30 years, for a long time, for a large portion of his adult life.

He nods and says, "Sure, but there are so many people who have it worse than I do."

Leola speaks up. "We have each other. We really get along so well and enjoy each other's company. And we have a lot of fun playing cards. We play with our friends every week."

Jud says. "And we enjoy nature. We really enjoy the birds. We get about ten kinds out here. See, right there's a chickadee. The house finches are *still* trying to figure out how to use that goldfinch feeder!"

It was one October Jud and Leola found they yet had quite a few blueberries and raspberries that needed to be used.

"I like to have a glass of wine before dinner," says Jud. "That's OK for me, isn't it?... Well, here we had all these berries and I wanted to make some wine out of them. But see, wine takes six months to make. I didn't know... would I be around that long? Would I be here to drink it?"

"So what did you do?"

"Well, we went ahead and made the wine. My youngest daughter, Jan, and I did it together. A few weeks ago we tried a little, just to see, and we added some sugar. It should be ready by spring. Now I'm looking forward to sitting right out there," he points out the window to the deck, "and having my wine."

Not in the least afraid of death, Jud and Leola speak of being here or not being here in a matter of fact way. Having found joy in simple things, and with faith as solid as a rock, they sit back now and savor each day of their life together. Serenely steadfast and wise, they talk of the coming season with hope.

See picture, page 74

Jud and Leola share devotions each day.
This is Jud's favorite passage.

"The Lord is my Shepherd: I shall not want.
He makes me to lie down in green pastures; he leads me beside the still waters.
He restores my soul: he leads me in the paths of righteousness for his name's sake.
Yea, though I walk through the valley of the shadow of death, I will fear no evil: for thou art with me; thy rod and thy staff, they comfort me.
Thou preparest a table before me in the presence of mine enemies; thou anointest my head with oil; my cup runneth over.
Surely goodness and mercy shall follow me all the days of my life; and I will dwell in the house of the Lord forever."

Psalm 23

No Time for Feeling Down

Marian

"Do not let it get the best of you.
Worry only increases the breathing problems.
Force yourself to change your lifestyle to one less strenuous."
Nina Caiozzo, Shelby Township, MI

Whether or not we are faced with limitations in breathing, we can all find inspiration in Marian's optimistic outlook. This is the story of Marian Hyde, a big lady with a big heart and a warm, friendly smile.

"Life is great and I look forward to everyday. I do not allow myself to be mad at anyone or feel down about anything."

Marian was born in Allegan, Michigan at the end of the Great Depression into a large family of seven children, three boys and four girls. Though everyone in the family worked hard, theirs was a happy life, full of good-natured teasing and laughter. Marian loved school. It was her social life.

Having a mother with asthma and Marian herself having problems with allergies did not seem like a big deal to her as she was growing up. Breathing was not a problem. Smoking her first cigarette at age ten seemed just fine to her. After all, it was the cool thing to do. Back then, in the 1940's, it seemed like everyone she knew smoked.

In her 50's, however, Marian started noticing difficulty breathing. She did herself a big favor by quitting smoking, but some damage had been done. It was not until two years later that she was diagnosed with chronic bronchitis. Her physician then prescribed allergy shots and metered dose inhalers (MDI's). As a result of these treatments there was a great improvement in Marian's breathing. Everything seemed fine now. She was feeling well and enjoying her job in employee relations at a large pharmaceutical company.

"My problems really started when I suddenly came up with a bleeding ulcer caused by medication. This lead to another, very urgent situation—one day I could not catch my breath! I can only describe this feeling as the most helpless, hopeless feeling in the world.

"I went for help to our small local hospital in South Haven, Michigan. I was only getting worse, so from there I was taken to a larger hospital in St. Joseph, Michigan. It was then found that I had a number of blood clots in my lungs. I knew exactly how serious this was. Only eight months earlier I had lost a very dear sister who died from blood clots in her lungs. I remained at that hospital, in critical care for two days. But my condition continued to worsen. They told me there wasn't anything they could do for me.

"Was I scared? No, I was not afraid. Somehow I *knew* I was not going to die. This was just something I had to go through. It was during this time that I felt a special kind of peace like I had never known before. I didn't share the worry or fear of the people around me; my family who never left my side, or the doctors and nurses. When this peace came, any fear that might have been there, was gone.

"As a last chance, I was taken by ambulance to a large university hospital in Ann Arbor, Michigan. I found out later that there were some who thought I might not live long enough to reach there. I was in the critical care unit in Ann Arbor for another eight days. In that time I had 14 blood transfusions and 24 hour oxygen at 10 liters per minute.

"I was also tested for sleep apnea [a dangerous decrease or absence of breathing during sleep]. The result of the sleep test was positive and I started sleeping with the help of a CPAP machine. This began to help improve the low oxygen level in my blood.

"After the sixth day in Ann Arbor I finally began to improve. The bleeding stopped. The blood oxygen level was climbing and the blood clots seemed to be dissolving. After two more days I was released and went home with 24 hour a day liquid oxygen at 6 liters per minute."

It was at this time that Marian was referred to Pulmonary Rehabilitation. She came in the first day, short of breath, tired and weak. Her short reddish-brown hair was fringed by beads of perspiration from the work she had just done—the work of walking from her car into the building. Marian's multiple health problems concerned the staff. Not only did she have COPD, she also suffered from sleep apnea, arthritis, chronic back pain, pulmonary hypertension (high blood pressure in the vessels in the lungs), and a strain on her heart caused by the COPD and her weight.

But Marian was eager to start the rehab program! She was prepared to do everything she could to get stronger and to learn all she could about how to breathe better. Throughout Marian's eight-week involvement in the program, she came faithfully to class not only ready to work and learn, but also inclined to smile, laugh, and have fun with staff and her new found friends. She worked so hard, riding the bike and walking on the treadmill, even though sometimes feeling pain in her back, she would smile and encourage a classmate. As a result of her participation Marian had what she described as a "tremendous" increase in the activities she was able to do at home. She felt much better. But, as impressive as this was, Marian did more than just help herself in rehab. Her cheerful presence each day was a lift, a *joyful gift*, to all.

Each person who comes to Pulmonary Rehab is asked what their goals are; things they'd like to be able to do as a result of their participation in the program or things they would like to see as a change in their lives. One of Marian's goals was to be able to stop using supplemental oxygen completely. She was unable to achieve that goal by the end of the eight weeks, but graduated from the program determined to keep working toward it.

"Three months later I went back to Ann Arbor for a check up. The oxygen was lowered to two liters per minute and only needed when I was active. At that point I was released to the care of my local doctor. I truly believe that someday, especially if I lose a substantial amount of weight, I won't need extra oxygen at all. Recently it was confirmed that I have rheumatoid arthritis. This makes weight loss a little harder because of the lack of exercise. It's happening slowly—but it is happening."

Nearly losing her life, struggling with so many other health concerns—what keeps Marian optimistic in spite of all the negatives?

"I am accepting of my condition because I feel grateful that I'm this well. I know there are so many others in worse condition than I am and I admire their strength.

"Every place I go people approach me and ask about the oxygen. Sometimes they just give me an all-knowing nod and ask, 'Are you an ex-smoker?' Others will look at me and say, 'What is it, emphysema?' So often someone asks me about the liquid oxygen because its something they are not familiar with. I have talked to so many people about my breathing problem and they in turn have told me their story. It has been good therapy for me, and I hope it has been good for them.

"My sister says if you're not on oxygen or holding a baby, no one talks to you. I have noticed she has started using her cane again. People hold doors for me. I notice my sister stays close so she can go through too. The best thing of all, though, is when people smile at me. It makes me feel good."

What helps Marian get through each day with her lung disease?

"Physically, exercise helps. Another very important thing I've learned through this experience is that if it is a hard breathing day it is OK to slow down and even rest if needed.

"Emotionally, I find help in using the relaxation tape I received in Pulmonary Rehab and in the support of my family.

"Spiritually, I have found an inner peace with myself, with other people, and with the world.

"When asked if she could say one thing to somebody with chronic lung disease who is about to give up, Marian's response is, "This too shall pass. Find something to enjoy every day, no matter how small it might be."

Marion Hyde

Sheila

"Do something to help someone."
Jeanette Van Kley, South Holland, IL

Some people with Chronic Lung Disease find it helpful to put their feelings down on paper. Through the hardship and frustration of living with shortness of breath, come stories, letters and poems. Just the act of writing them down, it seems, can provide help, calmness, and perspective. Sharing them with another person benefits both.

Sheila Shiel is an active member of an on line COPD support group. She is always there with an encouraging word to a member of the group who is struggling on a bad day, or to answer a question if she can. In spite of many problems with her health, Sheila gives of herself to lift others up, always finishing her note with the words, "Think Rainbows and Smile."

"COPD makes a good subject to write about in a human interest sort of way. I can write about the loneliness of the disease, the ups and downs due to the

46

medications, the tendency for some of us to "hide" because of the difficulty going out and facing the world, the over-reaction to being Short of Breath (SOB), and the tendency to want to just chill out when feeling good because of the fear of becoming ill again. Add to this the smoking aspect—not all COPD is due to smoking—yet everybody asks you about smoking no matter who or what. Then there are the day-to-day difficulties of just taking a shower, eating a meal, trying to cope, and so on.

"COPD is not a nice disease. Sometimes I get depressed. I wrote quite a lot one summer when I was ill. My poems tell a personal story about the ups and downs of having COPD."

Sheila Shiel

I Was Dreaming

I woke up this morning tasting food ... things I used to eat.
Lots of sauce and red meat,
Pies and homemade bread and things I used to make.
Opened my eyes ... I was in bed, for goodness sake!

I dreamed that I was walking on the beach,
No cane, no pain, walking with my head up high to reach ...
the sky.
My, oh, my.

In my dream, I was so alive and carefree ...
The way I used to be.

I closed my eyes and went back to sleep ...
I wanted to hold on to my memories,
have something to keep!

I know I have to face reality ...
But sometimes I close my eyes just to see ...
A young and healthy me!

Crying

Why do I feel these tears tonight?
When everything was going alright?
Is this part of what I have to face for the rest of my Life ...
What's left of my Life, that is ...
for I don't know ...
How much time before
God brings me Home.

Up and down I go.
First I am happy and gay,
Living and enjoying every single day.
Then suddenly I feel so low ...
Where did that happiness go?

All part of this terrible disease.
So hard to believe
That one day you are so high ...
Wondering if you can fly?
Next day you hit that horrible low ...
A kick in the stomach, a terrible blow.
Tears run down my face ... and I cry ...
I don't even know why ...

Think Pink

Think Pink ... You can win!
Life can be happy and gay,
Depends on how you want to spend your day.

Lots of hardship, lots of pain ...
It is part of God's game.
Smile and go on and just look for my rainbow in the sky ...
Soon you will be feeling just fine.

See the moon and the starts at night.
Hug yourself really tight.
Smile with all your might.
Everything is a-okay, alright?

Love is something you keep inside and give out when you
have to ...
Always remember the one to Love the most is YOU.

Full Moon Fantasy

They found a cure for COPD today.
It has finally come our way.

You take a pill and your lungs become all brand new,
Once again ... you can breathe like you used to do!

Bronchitis is a thing of the past,
No more coughing and meds that don't last.
No more gasping for breath.

Emphysema, too, has become a thing of the past.
Nobody needs new lungs or any other type of surgical
intervention.
They finally researched and paid attention ...
to our plight.
We won the fight!

Cigarettes have been abolished forever ... nobody smokes
anymore,
All lung diseases have been cured.

It was only a dream ... another
Full Moon Fantasy,
But oh, I wish it were really true ... so I could be
the way I used to be … able to breathe.

I walked on the beach today,
Felt the wind and sunshine on my face.
I walked for miles and miles with my toes sunk into the sand.
It felt so grand.

And in the morning I got dressed all by myself,
No treatment, no oxygen, I didn't need any help.

Another Full Moon Fantasy ... as tears run down my face ...
As I suck in my O$_2$ and dream that things are truly that way.

Hoping that someday soon ... they may.

COPD links are available on our website at:
www.breathingbetterlivingwell.com

www.lungusa.org

www.COPD-International.com

www.Pulmonarypaper.org

www.thebreathingspace.com

www.emphysema.net

www.aarc.org

www.buyersguide.aarc.org

www.breethezy.com

www.njh.org

www.goldcopd.com

www.coloradohealthsite.org

www.nhlbi.nih.gov/health/public/lung/other/copd/

Section Three

Asthma

"Find a good doctor, a specialist if necessary,
then take good advice and use it."
Justine Reiger, Warren, MI

A Normal Life

Janet

"Keep trying.
New treatments are being found.
Go to the meetings.
You'll find many people to encourage you."

Janet Van Dommelen is a tireless crusader for effective asthma management, and she has reason to be. She is living proof that a person with severe asthma can live a normal, symptom-free life. As I was putting together names of asthma experts to speak at our annual Asthma Day event, it was suggested that the panel include a patient's perspective. Immediately I thought of Janet. Who better to talk about what optimal management can do to improve life for those with asthma than somebody who had experienced the highs and lows, and triumphed over this disease?

Janet was suffering that day from laryngitis and was very nervous about speaking to the large group. But undaunted, she walked up to the podium and told her story. Although Janet's voice was weak, the audience heard every

54

word. Everybody was touched by her story and by the quiet confidence with which she gave hope for people with asthma to live a normal life.

Today Janet continues to practice excellent compliance with her asthma management plan and reaches out whenever she can to help others find that life with asthma can get better! Here, in her own words, is what she shared with the Asthma Day audience.

"Thank you for giving me the opportunity to share with you today. I am not a public speaker, although my family assures me that I love to talk! I consider it to be an honor and a privilege that I have been invited to share my passion, which has become my success story; because my life with asthma is that—a tale of success.

"I was in the 10th grade when, after playing field hockey, I discovered some wheezing problems. Although I was symptomatic, the condition did not seem serious. My pediatrician gave me pills that enabled me to keep active.

"Some years later, after getting married, the problems gradually intensified. Not that it was my husband's fault, understand! Actually, his compassion made things easier, especially when I began to require inhalers and strong medications that affected my emotions, my sleep cycle, my whole life. After some time I knew I was in real trouble. I made emergency room trips approximately every three months. At that time, I began spending most of my summers in my bedroom. Without central air, the window unit in our bedroom made that room the only comfortable place in our home. I would cook and do laundry, but only in short installments, returning to the comfort of the bedroom, sometimes with the family joining me there at mealtime.

"At the time we didn't know anyone else with asthma, much less severe asthma, and so it seemed difficult for others to understand what was going on. I finally discovered that by having my family and a friend to support me, I could manage. However, I really think the ability to share with others in support groups is extremely important. Being misunderstood is a frequent experience for asthma patients—and I felt continually criticized by others who didn't understand that asthma sometimes acts unpredictably—things that might trigger an attack one day might not the next, and so forth. For me, even opening the freezer door might trigger an episode.

"Another frustration of this period of my life was the uncertainty. I simply could not make concrete plans. Some Sundays I regretted having to send off my kids and husband to church and being unable to join them. Many times I would plan to go somewhere or do something, only to be forced to change plans when my health became problematic. This was a very lonely time.

"We eventually installed central air, and that was, as you would think, a factor that brought change. Unfortunately, the change was for the worse—not for the better. I really regressed at this point, finding it so difficult to breathe at times that I would need to be rushed to the hospital for a shot of adrenaline, IV's and, breathing treatments so that my lungs could find a way to stabilize. I know now that in that time period my symptoms were being treated—but the underlying inflammation was not. Let me stop here to emphasize that no matter how bad your asthma is, it is a reversible disease. Asthma *can* be treated. I knew this, even in the low points. I would pray and have hope even though I couldn't understand why I was getting worse.

"About this time, I was preparing with my family to go on vacation, although I knew that much of my time would be spent in the motel. I called my doctor's office asking if my appointment could be moved up since I wasn't doing well. The nurse told me that a new doctor had joined the practice and that my physician wanted me to see this new lung specialist. What transpired as a result of that meeting with my Pulmonary Specialist is—to me—truly miraculous. It turned my life around!

"First, my new doctor explained to me about treatment options. There were new discoveries about asthma and new medications that would now treat the underlying problem—*the inflammation*. He also made sure that whenever there was a problem I was to call him. Next, he introduced me to a peak flow meter. This device is an important indicator of lung function. When you blow into the meter, it measures the speed at which your air goes out. Daily peak flow readings can help detect subtle changes in your lung function— sometimes even before you are aware of them.

"Then, after a while my asthma was under control. By this time, having gotten to know me, and knowing my needs and abilities, my doctor worked out with me a written asthma management plan. He told me that he would teach me to be my own asthma doctor—learning from him 'effective asthma management'—ways I can help myself keep my own asthma under control.

"One aspect of this doctor's success, for me, was that he never assumed at first that I knew how to follow through on his instruction. Even though I had been on inhalers for years, my doctor showed me how to use them—and then had me demonstrate to his satisfaction—that I knew how to use them correctly. Proper usage enabled me to gain the maximum amount of medication from each inhaler. He walked through the treatment plan with me to make sure I wouldn't fail! And, as you can see, I didn't! Through all this he made sure I understood that he would be there for me whenever I needed encouragement or teaching and, of course, his *direct* management.

"Today, I am a totally different person. I am virtually without symptoms. I live a normal life. I make advance plans, and I carry them through to completion. I'm out of the bedroom. Now I only sleep there! I enjoy taking neighborhood walks—even on somewhat humid days.

"My family and friends, and even those who previously were unable to understand, now see a new level of health and involvement, and they recognize the impact of my 'doctoring.' For you see, an asthma patient and his or her lung specialist make quite a team. I call us the medical miracle! Or, in my case, my own story of hope and success.

"I would like to take advantage of this opportunity to thank publicly those who have been instrumental in my life with asthma. Thank you to the facilitators of the Better Breathers' Club. You have encouraged and educated each of us.

"Thank you to the wonderful man I married—the man who loved me when my emotions changed my personality due to King Kong doses of steroids. You often knew what was better for me that I did myself. I love you, Don!

"Then to you, my doctor, for your part in my recovery—and for bringing me to a life of normalcy.

"Lastly, to you asthma patients, I have some challenges in the form of questions. Are you a slave to your asthma? Are you able to take that wonderful walk you always used to enjoy? What about that great bike ride? How long has it been since you have taken one? Think about it.

"My advice to you: Don't hesitate to call back if the current plan isn't helping. Your doctor will have additional ideas. Remember, follow your doctor's instructions, explicitly, always! Just because you may be feeling well, don't omit medications on your own. These medications are probably the very reason you are doing well!

"Sometimes you will need medication adjustments, but let your doctor make these decisions. Treatment is individualized. Remember, there is no treatment plan that works for everyone. Following the instructions of a doctor knowledgeable in the treatment of asthma *will* result in success!

"Finally, NEVER, NEVER GIVE UP!"

Janet and Don Van Dommelen

Asthma Facts

- Asthma is a Chronic Lung Disease characterized by inflammation or swelling of the airways and increased responsiveness to asthma triggers.

- It is estimated that over 14 million people in the United States have asthma.

- More than 5,600 people die of asthma in the U.S. every year. That is 15 deaths every day, and represents an increase of 45% in mortality between 1985 and 1995. The death rate for African-Americans is almost three times that of Caucasians.

- Among chronic illnesses in children, asthma is the most common. Approximately 33% of asthma patients are under the age of 18.

His Mission of Music

Juke

"You can live better with Pulmonary Rehabilitation and the right advice."
Betty Roemer, Detroit, MI

Juke Ver Hoef is a dear man. Physically, he moves pretty fast, he tends to dart around a room, if not with his whole body, with his eyes. Juke spent much of his life as a carpenter, and when he joined us in Rehab, he was still working part time doing small cabinetry jobs. He is quick with a strong hug or to hold a person's face in his hands as one would a grandchild. Here is his story told in his own words, of his life with asthma and bronchitis, and of his new-found mission.

"I had always enjoyed singing in the choir but my breathing had become increasingly difficult. Because of this I thought I would not be able to sing much longer. I decided at the age of 71 to sing a solo, my first one. The response of the people at church was overwhelming. They thought I should have started this

61

20 years ago! Their encouragement launched me into a singing career. I decided then that I would sing as long as my breathing held out.

"A few years later my daughter-in-law suggested that I should go to the *Better Breathers' Club* to learn more about my problem. So I did. One of the speakers was a lady from St. Joseph, Michigan, who told about her double lung transplant. She had progressed from being totally confined in a wheelchair to winning bicycling races. She strongly recommended the Pulmonary Rehab program at our local hospital, an eight-week course (two days a week, two hours a day). Her enthusiasm and encouragement were just what I needed. Although I thought it was quite a commitment, I did sign up for the program.

"My first five weeks were the toughest. I felt that I was getting worse and my wife agreed. But the staff at Rehab promised, 'We are going to help you feel better. Trust us and just keep going.' At the end of the eight weeks I knew they were right. It was a terrific change! To my greatest surprise I could not only breathe easier, but I found that I had a new stronger singing voice. Praise God!

"Now I not only sing in my church, but anywhere else I can. I am part of a small group that brings inspirational entertainment to area nursing homes each month. This gives me many opportunities to sing solos and also lead the hymn singing.

"The Lord has provided these wonderful opportunities for me even at the age of 76! Surely he had a plan for my life when He directed me to these different organizations for healing. To thank Him I gladly use my voice to proclaim His greatness, His power and His wonderful love for me."

Juke Ver Hoef

A Winning Season

Jennifer

*"Acceptance gives you the power to acquire knowledge.
Knowledge gives you the power to fight."*

Jennifer Smith, a college student and award-winning tennis player, was also invited to share her story at our annual Asthma Day event. She captivated the audience with her youthful energy and her story of courage and victory. Now married and living in Ohio, Jennifer Lane teaches French and coaches tennis. She exercises nearly every day and takes tap lessons. Her husband and she love to travel and are planning a bike trip. Jennifer says, "Asthma no longer hinders me in any way from enjoying everyday life or experiencing new things."

"Thanks for inviting me to share my story with you. It is truly a privilege.

"In my freshman year of college, there were several occasions on which I had difficulty breathing when

when I was playing tennis, but I brushed it off as being out of shape. However, the problems persisted to the point where I had to stop in the middle of competition because I could not breathe well. I was *afraid* because I did not understand why this was happening. I was *confused* because I had been playing competitive tennis for eight years and was a three-sport athlete in high school. *Why now?* I was *concerned* because I had never had a problem like this before, and now I was concerned enough to seek medical assistance.

"I went to my primary care doctor who diagnosed the breathing problems as allergy related, thus I was referred to an allergist. After my visit to the allergist, I was diagnosed with exercise-induced asthma. I was shocked! How could this be happening to me? Thoughts and fears of not being able to exercise or to play tennis in college or *ever* being able play again, began to race through my head. *Was this the end of my athletic career?*

"I soon discovered that I was not the only one with asthma but that thousands of people and athletes have it and manage it successfully. I also realized that this was not the end of my tennis career but rather with the proper medication and by following simple management strategies, I could continue to compete. I also began to reflect on my past and realized that I had experienced the warning signs of asthma long before now. For example, I would often get extremely short of breath during conditioning, wind sprints, and long distance running. I also had a job, which exposed me to harsh chemicals and caused me to experience severe breathing problems and illness. As a result of the intense strain, my pulmonary track was much weaker than before.

"The idea of having asthma was so very foreign to me and initially I really struggled to understand how to use all the new medications I was taking. I was also very embarrassed about having to use my inhalers when I played because I felt like I was showing my opponent a weakness. I tried to be very discrete so that no one would know I needed an inhaler.

"Once I had accepted my diagnosis, it was a challenge for me to learn how to live with asthma, but I slowly became more sensitive to my body and my medications. I was put on several inhalers: one to prevent inflammation and another to stop breathing problems when they occurred. The regimen I had established worked very well for me until the fall of my junior year when my health started to steadily deteriorate. I was having difficulty breathing and, well, even functioning for that matter. Nothing was making me feel better.

"So I went back to the allergist and was tested for allergies. They quickly discovered that I was severely allergic (like off the charts allergic!) to everything on their list except for dogs, saline and feathers—at least there are three things in this world! As a result, I started on some new medications, took steps to reduce the allergens surrounding me, and started allergy shots.

"Unfortunately I still was not getting better. In fact, I was getting worse. It got to the point where I could not function at the normal daily level. I was experiencing a lot of fatigue, chest pain, and had difficulty breathing, preventing me from attending classes, playing tennis and going about everyday life. My lowest of lows came one day in early February when I was playing a tennis match and had to default because I had an asthma attack on the court. This was very upsetting for me because it happened in front of all my teammates who were equally as scared and concerned as I was. I was also upset that I was forced to quit and I felt like I had lost control over the functioning of my body. *I had hit my rock bottom point and right then and there I decided that I was going to beat this thing before it beat me. I was going to take control again of my body and my life!*

"After some persistence on my part I was finally referred to a pulmonologist in March and started on a myriad of new medications the week of our spring break tennis trip. It was he, the lung specialist, who taught me how to use a peak flow meter and to record my daily progress on peak flow charts. Even though this seemed foreign to me, I now had the tools I needed to succeed. All I had to do was follow through. I realized that carrying out his instructions was necessary for me to make progress and at that point I was willing to do *anything* in order to get better.

"I became a lot less shy about people around me knowing I had asthma for both their sake and mine and, in fact, it soon became my desire to educate them. I wanted others to know what was going on in my body because what you don't understand you are more inclined to fear. So I decided to explain to my college housemates and teammates what asthma was, what it was doing to my body and how they should react if an emergency situation arose.

"I began doing all my peak flows and meds in the bathroom, which I shared with six other girls. One day one of them said to me, 'Not doing so hot today, huh?'

"I replied, 'How do you know?'

"She said, 'Well, when you do well you always say 'yessss!' after your peak flow reading—and when you do poorly you always do a deep sigh.'

"I guess you can say I'm competitive!

"Managing my asthma was also an education process for me to learn about myself, to learn about my triggers, to know about my body and how it reacts, knowing when to increase or decrease my medications, and how to take proactive steps to prevent asthma episodes. I was like a sponge and read everything I could get my hands on about asthma so I could better understand what was going on in my body.

"I went back to my pulmonologist after a month of this treatment and brought my peak flow charts. I had diligently completed all sides and columns daily, just as he had asked. The charts graphically showed my roller coaster-like start, but with my commitment and dedication to follow the regimen, I had achieved consistently high peak flow results. It is true that I experienced many ups and downs and it has been far from easy, but it has been well worth the effort. By bringing my charts with me, the doctor could better treat me because he could see my daily progress. This said a lot more to him than, 'Oh yeah, I'm doing better,' when he asked me how I was feeling.

"My breathing had been indeed out of control and but now I am happy to say that it is under control. I went from defaulting matches in February of my junior year in college to having one of my most successful tennis seasons ever by the end of April. I was named First Team All-Conference two years running, league MVP, and finished my college career ranked 14th in the nation in Division III tennis! I still remember the day when I thought all my athletic dreams had been lost, but I remind myself that it was possible to do what I first thought impossible.

"Through this I began to appreciate things I had taken for granted. Breathing and exercise became a privilege. I learned that just because you are given medication, it will not fully help you unless you are determined to take it and not stop taking it even if you feel better. Asthma control is maximized with preventative measures so that instead of putting out fires, you simply make sure that one never occurs.

"If you suffer from asthma, I encourage you to view your doctor as a teammate. He or she will help you regulate your medication if you provide the information needed. Having a good asthma doctor and working in partnership with him brought about a night and day change to my health and I know that steps like these can, *and will*, do the same for yours."

Jennifer (back row, third from right) with her team

Jennifer on the court

Jennifer Lane with her husband, Brian

Goals for Asthma Patients

Don't settle for less!
A person with asthma should expect the following:

- No emergency room visits due to asthma

- No overnight hospital stays because of asthma

- No missed school or work due to asthma

- Normal or near normal level of physical activity

- No interruptions in sleep from coughing or shortness of breath

- Use of rescue / reliever inhaler minimal, less than two times a week or only pre-exercise.

There is Much Joy in Life

Leola

"Say a daily prayer."

In many cases a spouse can empathize but never fully understand what his or her partner is going through. Leola Johnson (the wife of Justin who we met in the COPD section) also has Chronic Lung Disease. Although her younger years were not fraught with pulmonary hazards as were her husband's, Leola has had her share of trouble breathing.

When she was about 60 years old Leola developed bronchitis leading to an asthma attack, a visit to the emergency room, and overnight hospital stay. Asthma? *At her age?* She thought this must just be an isolated episode. After discharge she denied for about six weeks that there would ever be any further problems. But her asthma attacks continued becoming more and more serious.

One Thanksgiving night around ten o'clock Leola had a terrible asthma attack. She had been coughing hard all day. The family, gathered together for the holiday noticed that their mom was having trouble. But none of them ever suspected that asthma could get so bad. Later in the day, with all the guests gone, and with night coming on, Leola's airways were getting tighter and tighter. She was working harder and harder to breathe. Jud knew it was time to get help, so they got into the car and started off to the hospital. On their way, Jud noticed that his wife's breathing was getting even worse. Suddenly Leola said aloud, "**Lord, help me**," and stopped breathing. Her skin was blue. Jud was driving 80 MPH down the country roads, slowing down just enough at intersections to avoid other cars. By the time they reached the hospital Leola was in full arrest, with no breathing and no heart beat. The emergency entrance area was under construction at that time and the staff member assigned to that door was busy with another emergency. Jud was helped at the front door that night by a stranger, a visitor to the hospital, who helped him get his wife to the emergency room.

Leola was revived, transferred to the critical care unit and connected to a ventilator that breathed for her. For two days she did not respond. Jud was afraid he might lose Leola, his dear wife and soul mate. He also faced the possibility that if she did recover, because of the possible lack of oxygen, she might never be the same person he knew.

After ten days in the hospital Leola was discharged, expected to make a full recovery! She credits her faith in God and her family's concern with helping her to go on.

Always together, Leola and Justin attended Pulmonary Rehabilitation and found that there was a lot to learn about taking care of their lungs and their overall health.

Today Leola gets through her days by carefully pacing her activities. At times she finds comfort in speaking words of encouragement to herself, and even shedding tears.

When asked what has changed the most after diagnosis, struggling with shortness of breath and near death, Leola responds, "The appreciation of life and family." She reminds herself "there is much joy in life, especially if you have grandchildren, children and a spouse."

When her children ask her what they should pray for, Leola's simple request: "Pray for Dad's health and that I can cope with the day."

Jud and Leola share devotions every day. Here is a passage especially meaningful to her.

> *"Believe on the name of the Son of God; that you may know that you have eternal life, and that you may believe on the name of the Son of God." 1 John 5: 13b*

Justin and Leola Johnson

Asthma Resources

www.aafa.org
Asthma and Allergy Foundation of America

www.aanma.org
Allergy and Asthma Network / Mothers of Asthmatics

www.aaaai.org
American Academy of Allergy, Asthma, and Immunology

www.aafa.org
Allergy and Asthma Foundation of America

www.ibreathe.com
Glaxo Smith Kline

www.breatheinfo.com
Astra Zeneca

www.asthma.org.uk/
National Asthma Campaign

www.lungusa.org
American Lung Association

www.njh.org
National Jewish Hospital

www.dallasasthma.org
Dallas Asthma Consortium

Section Four

Alpha-1 Antitrypsin Deficiency

"It may not be easy, but you can live a full life.
Keep active. Exercise. Volunteer."
Leo F. Hobbs, Roseville, MI

Accept Your Challenge, Take Responsibility, Live Well!

Mary

"Live each day at a time. Make the most of your time."
John Kennedy, West Olive, MI

I knew of Mary Pierce and her experience and had even met her once when she so graciously agreed to drive from St. Joseph, Michigan 60 miles North to Holland to speak at a meeting of our Better Breathers' Club. On that snowy February afternoon Mary told her inspiring story to our group of about thirty people with Chronic Lung Disease. She shared with us the account of her battle with A-1AD (Alpha-1 Antitrypsin Deficiency, an inherited form of emphysema, striking people in their 20's, 30's, 40's, and 50's) and her devastating decline in health. She spoke of her search for appropriate nutritional support and finally of her recovery following a double lung transplant, only the ninth such operation in the State of Michigan as of April 1999. She also shared news of her formidable accomplishments since her transplant operation.

Indeed Mary's story of her return to health is amazing. Through hardship and even desperation, Mary taught herself how to use every available resource to regain her health. I visited her in her home to interview her for this book and expected to hear of her experience in more detail; but nothing I'd heard, read or researched prepared me for her deep insight, her resourcefulness, boundless courage, and generous spirit.

As I was getting out of my car that day in May, Mary greeted me with a strong handshake and a warm smile. She appeared healthy and athletic, wearing black slacks and shirt and silver jewelry. We entered her home, a quiet, peaceful place on the St. Joseph River. The weather report that day called for dreary skies and rain. But as we sat in the family room with its views of river and woods, talk was anything but dull. I sat down and didn't get up for almost four hours as Mary told me her story. Our conversation was peppered with phone calls from AlphaNet patients calling Mary, an AlphaNet Coordinator, but I didn't mind. Hearing Mary counsel each person—patient helping patient—was an inspiration to me. Immersed in this environment, even for a short while, I was only beginning to grasp of the level of caring and commitment in the heart of each Alpha.

"Everybody isn't going to have a lung transplant, that's for sure. But living with Chronic Lung Disease should be something like wringing out a dishrag. You've got to wring *every bit* of life out of what you've got. There are many tools to help you get the most quality out of the life you've got left. If you choose not to have a transplant you can still make that next five years... there's a way that you can make the best out of those five years. You *can* do it because it means the difference between sitting in your chair with your oxygen and wishing you could get out and do something, or getting yourself into shape the best you can, in spite of your awful lungs. It can mean going to the park with your grand kids or doing whatever it is that gives you joy. Take what you have right now and work with that. Don't expect a magic bullet to do it for you."

Mary Pierce had never heard of Alpha-1 Antitrypsin Deficiency before she was diagnosed. She recalls having gotten a couple of "really serious lung infections," but she considered herself to be in good health. After all, she was playing tennis right up until the time she graduated from college at age 30.

"I didn't take much notice of shortness of breath, the first obvious symptom. Over the next few years I had a few bouts of really bad bronchitis, maybe even pneumonia. I'd go to a clinic, to a doctor I didn't know and I'd get expectorants and antibiotics. I always had sort of a smoker's cough, just like my mother. I thought I'd just cough like this forever, but the people at work thought I was dying. I'd head to the bathroom and I'd just cough and cough and cough. Then I began to lose weight. Having always been about 20 pounds overweight, I thought this was great."

Over the next ten years, Mary continued to lose more weight. It was during this time she had changed jobs and had a lot of stress, and also began the long process of realizing that something was very wrong with her breathing.

One time a friend of hers came to visit from California. It was this friend's idea to go play tennis. After running for just three balls Mary was in trouble.

She remembers thinking, *"Hey, what's going on here? I can't breathe!"*

At that point Mary could not admit having breathing difficulties to herself, let alone to her friend.

"I faked it and said, 'It's really too hot, let's not play.'"

Looking back, it was that experience that Mary says really hit her between the eyes. Nevertheless, it would be quite a long time before she would face her disease. Her reason for not playing tennis that day was just one in a long line of excuses for why she could not do what healthy people usually find easy. This failure to face the facts and the truth was in spite of the fact that she was all too familiar with Chronic Lung Disease. Mary's dad died of emphysema and her mom of lung cancer and emphysema. Her husband's father had also died of lung cancer and emphysema.

With a deep sigh Mary said, "I know what it looks like."

Mary's parents had both smoked cigarettes. She recalls aunts and uncles coming over to play cards and the house being full of cigarette smoke. She herself started smoking at about age 13, sneaking cigarettes.

"When I started getting symptoms, mainly the weight loss and shortness of breath, I thought, "You dummy, you've got to stop this. No doctor's going to be able to do anything for you until you do this [quit smoking] for yourself."

Over the next ten years Mary took several stop smoking classes. Although she cut down on cigarettes (to around a half a pack per day), she continued to smoke. And her breathing wasn't getting any better.

As the years went by, Mary was *still* losing weight and hiding her increasing shortness of breath from her family, friends, and co-workers.

"I was doing everything I could to pretend that it was OK. I hardly wanted to admit it to myself."

Her job as a CPA for a large heavy equipment company required her to do a lot of traveling with her co-workers. She found herself on an airplane or in an airport more often than not. Walking through the airport was a real problem. By this time Mary, like so many chronic lung patients who are in

81

denial, had gotten very clever at concealing her symptoms. She would tell the others with whom she was traveling that she had to go to the bathroom and say she'd catch up with them. She did this simply because she could not keep up with the group, and would later struggle at her own pace to meet them.

In spite of this extreme shortness of breath and overall decline in health Mary still hung on to that first morning cigarette.

"I smoked one cigarette a day. I couldn't give that one up."

It was becoming more and more difficult for her to breathe. She had lost 50 pounds and gone from a size 14 to a size 6. Mary's weight now hovered around 105.

"I was skin and bone and I looked it. Not a healthy picture.

"At one point, I don't know when, I went to an ophthalmologist and he said, 'There's something really wrong with your breathing.' Again, I ignored it.

"I've got to quit smoking. Nothing's going to happen until I stop smoking.

"I just took all the responsibility. I'm a good Catholic girl. I took all the guilt on myself. I said to myself, 'Don't expect anybody else to help. I've got to do it my own dumb self. My smoking is doing it.' So that's how I rationalized it. What I didn't know was that because I was A-1AD deficient, my lungs lacked protection from the smoking. The damage was occurring at an accelerated pace. It was much more destructive to my lungs than it would have been to a person with normal lungs. I was developing the lungs of an old woman.

"Then one time I was all weekend sitting up, struggling to breathe in the chair, really struggling. I thought, 'Man, if I have to live like this I don't want to live anymore.'

"Monday morning came and I called the doctor. At that point I weighed 99 pounds. He took one look at me and said, 'You're too young to have this much lung disease.'"

That doctor called Mary a few days later on her 40th birthday, February 16, 1987, and said, "I was right. You have this thing called Alpha-1 Antitrypsin Deficiency. It's inherited. They're doing some experimental treatment at the NIH (National Institutes of Health). We can try to get you into a clinical trial."

"That gave me some hope.

"Then he said, 'They're also beginning to do lung transplants.'

"Transplants! *That's* the one thing that told me how bad it was." (At this point in time there had only ever been one lung transplant done on an Alpha patient in all of North America.)

"I can almost visualize myself standing in my kitchen, hanging the phone up, and saying to myself, 'OK, what do we do now? What do we do now to make this go away?'

"My husband, Todd, had done some literature research on lung disease on his father's behalf. He'd seen a story in a nursing magazine about a nurse who had helped her father's emphysema with nutritional changes. Nutritional help. I just needed to figure it out. That's all it took to send me off in that direction. I began buying books and reading about vitamins. I knew at that point that I was going to die of malnutrition before I died of lung disease. By then I had quit smoking, believe it or not, about four months before. I didn't feel any better and just continued to get worse. But I gradually began to add vitamins. I started reading

83

about all the vitamins, going right down the list, A, B, C, D... and started reading about complementary holistic kinds of things.

"I thought of it [treating severe lung disease] like having a quiver full of arrows. Each one was a weapon to use against this enemy, A-1AD. My weapons were knowledge, good nutrition, exercise, friends, family, sunshine, good books, peace, hope, and joy in small things. The effect was cumulative.

"Every day I'd get up in the morning and make myself a protein shake and increase the calories. I also bought an exercise bike and rode every day."

About a month later Mary went to see a local pulmonary doctor. The pulmonary function test revealed that her FEV_1 (the volume of air blown out in the first second of exhalation) was 14% of predicted (30% is considered severe, 25% considered disabled).

"I'll never forget it. I asked him, 'Is there anything I can do? Is there anything I can do nutritionally, exercise, whatever, to feel better?'

"He said, 'Nope, there's nothing you can do. Eat a good old American diet... and walk.'

"Remember, by now I'd done quite a bit of research. The walk part was probably good advice. But I'd expected at least a Pulmonary Rehab program or something.

"He said, 'You've got a chronic, inherited, ultimately fatal lung disease and there's nothing I can do about it.'

"I knew there were things *I* could do and that doctor was just not going to be in the equation.

"I later found a really good pulmonologist and he and I pretty much became partners. I'd advise anybody who is going to go through this to find a doctor who can be a partner, one who is willing to listen to you, answer questions and encourage you. A lot of the questions I had, my doctor really didn't like. I think he was concerned that in doing so much research about vitamin supplements I might mislead myself. But eventually he had some confidence that I wasn't going to go off half-cocked.

"In the meantime I'd written letters to all the nutritional associations. There were two huge books of listings I'd found in the library. In my letters I asked for referrals to doctors who had treated lung patients with nutrition. I finally got a response from a doctor at the NIH saying that there was a doctor in New York who would like to talk to me. I was given his phone number. So I called him up and he said, 'We'd love to see you.'

"In about a month Todd and I were driving East to see the nutritional doctors. Their office was two floors up. Todd and I walked up the stairs. These two doctors had seen all the X-rays and pulmonary function results and had expected me to be in a wheelchair, emaciated, barely able to breathe. When I'd told them I'd walked up the stairs they just couldn't believe it. They even separated Todd and me and interviewed each of us separately in order to make sure my story was true. After bringing us back together they sat us down and said, 'We don't know how you've done it, but you're on the right track. You've done what we're trying to do. But we think you've done all you can do orally [food by mouth] at this point.'"

"Then they told us about TPN."

Total Parenteral Nutrition was begun on Mary the next day by means of a tube, a subcutaneous catheter, inserted into the area just above her collar-bone and threaded into the large vein just above the heart. Mary and Todd stayed at a hotel near the doctors for two weeks and visited the office daily. It was there Mary and Todd learned sterile technique and how to infuse the special solution which was high in fat.

"The doctors made sure I knew precisely what I was doing before they sent us home to Michigan."

To understand how chronic obstructive pulmonary disease relates to nutrition and weight loss, it must be understood that breathing takes energy and calories. For most people breathing does not take a lot of energy, but for some people with chronic obstructive lung disease just breathing, and doing nothing else, can take all of the calories from the food eaten, and more. The more a person struggles to breathe, the more calories they need, and the more muscle they use. When a person is using more calories than he or she is taking in, the muscles become damaged and weak, and the person becomes malnourished. The diaphragm, the main muscle of breathing, is particularly stressed, being overworked and underfed. Factors common in many chronic lung disease patients such as decreased appetite, less energy for food preparation, and more energy expenditure in eating itself may be added, and then there is big trouble; a sure recipe for a continuing downward slide in health.

One way to help improve lung function in people is through diet. A high fat diet adds more weight per ounce and produces much less carbon dioxide than a diet higher in carbohydrates and sugars.[2] In Mary's case, she could not possibly eat enough to keep up with her respiratory demands. With an FEV_1 of 14 %, the TPN was the help she needed.

"Six months later tests showed that I was requiring about half the calories I had needed in the beginning to sustain my basic nutritional needs during rest. The TPN was working! My lung function leveled off and actually improved a bit. My muscles were in better shape. My diaphragm probably regained a little of its strength. Somehow I'd reduced my metabolic requirements."

Mary's case was so remarkable, it was published as an anecdotal case in the July / August 1992 issue of Nutrition, a medical journal for health care professionals. The article states that Mary's metabolic rate in the beginning required about 2400 calories per day. After six months of nutritional support with essential fatty acids, vitamins, and carbohydrates her metabolic rate had decreased to a level requiring about 1400 calories per day. A huge improvement.

Mary and her doctor, the Pulmonologist, knew that lung transplant was in her future, but at this point Mary wasn't even waiting for it.

"I was happy with the quality of my life. I was doing genealogical research. I was enjoying my house. Some of my most precious memories are of sitting over by that window in the sunshine with Sophie [her cat] on my lap, a [Gregorian] chant in the background, and a good book. I wasn't ready yet. Theoretically the best time might have been after I regained my nutritional status, but emotionally I wasn't ready to take that challenge on. But when the quality of my life diminished to the point where I felt it was just not worth it, that's when I made the decision to go on the list. I now know that decision has to be tempered with how long that wait is going to be, until a suitable organ becomes available. I waited too long.

"By then I had made all the adjustments mentally I'd needed to make. I'd gotten another lung infection and we knew the time had come. My doctor agreed and we said, 'Let's do it.' So we had the transplant evaluation and I was on the list.

"First visit at the transplant center, Dr. Lynch came in and brusquely said, 'OK, first of all, no double lungs.'"

"Todd said, 'That's no problem. Half a lung is just fine with us.'"

"I was thinking that it certainly would be lots more than I had.

"By then I was on oxygen full time. If we wanted to leave the house I had to use a wheelchair. We had ordered my own chair the morning I got my call from the transplant center at the University of Michigan. This was in April of 1993. I had been waiting on the transplant list for five months, since November.

"Due to the shortage of donated lungs, single lung transplants are most common for A-1AD patients. For some reason I was given two lungs. I have no idea who made the decision and why."

Since the transplant, Mary went on to win a Gold Medal in cycling at the World Transplant Olympics in 1995. She has also been a tireless advocate for Alpha-1 Antitrypsin Deficiency, actively promoting diagnosis and optimal care, as well as leading Team Alpha. A year after the Olympics she climbed Pike's Peak and attempted to top Mt. Rainier. In 1998 she cycled across the United States in the American Lung Association's Big Ride Across America. (See picture on page 211)

I asked Mary why she thinks she's done so exceptionally well following the transplant. "Since my surgery, yes, I've been doing very well. I think its luck, good lungs, good care, good docs, spiritual support. For some reason they [the lungs] were really compatible with me, or whatever... all that stuff. I think that's 50% of it. I think the other 50% is that I've worked very hard, exercised, and mostly watched my diet. I try not to worry much about my situation and remember every day that my life is a gift, a gift from a woman I'll never meet.

"I guess it just reminds me again that those things, proper diet and exercise, are extremely important to get the most out of life after a transplant. Those things are extremely important to get the most out of life if you're *not* going to get a transplant."

When I asked Mary "What is it that 'drives' her? To survive this, to ride, to do her work with AlphaNet?"

"What keeps driving me now is the patients. It's really pretty simple. I've learned a lot of things they're not going to hear anywhere else. I want them to have access to as much information as they can that will help them to get the most out of life that they can. I keep thinking about that dishrag. You know, you can wring it out a little bit and get a little bit, or you can REALLY wring it out and get every ounce of life that you can get out of it. All the little things that we can do to make our lives a little better, all of the arrows we put into the quiver, they really mean a lot for somebody with chronic lung disease. There isn't one *single* thing that's going to make a huge difference in anybody's life. Exercise by itself won't do it. Nutrition by itself won't do it. Education by itself won't do it. Music won't do it by itself, but when you add three or four or five of those little pieces together then we've got a huge improvement in the quality of life with chronic lung disease.

"You know, when I set out, all the reading I did told me I had 18 months to live, and I thought, 'Well, if that's it, that's it, but I want to make those 18 months as comfortable and as joyful and as productive as I can make them. I want to make those 18 months as *good* as they can be.'"

"Now I remind myself almost every day that I've been really blessed. I've been really lucky. I got... seven years? Gosh, it doesn't seem possible. It may go away tomorrow, but I'll die a happy camper, I guess, because I feel like I've made a contribution.

Her eyes well up as Mary quietly and reverently says, "If I ever met my donor family I could say I did my best with what they gave me."

"My hope is that the little bits and pieces I've spread will not end with the people who have picked them up, but will be shared with others and go even farther. I can just picture it: information and encouragement being shared by people and multiplying over and over to mean a better quality of life for so many. If each person who is helped even a little bit by what they've learned shares that with another, it will keep growing and growing.

"I'd love to see all chronic lung patients accept responsibility for making their lives whole, then go after it. It's about personal responsibility.

"Whatever it is that you're facing in your life, chronic lung disease, financial problems, marriage problems, whoever you are, you can't just sit back and leave it to fate, to other people to solve it for you. Too often in medical matters its too easy for us to go to the doctor and present him with our problem and expect him to take all the responsibility. That's not fair. It's not rational. We can get so much more if we get in there and have a partnership. Each partner, the patient and the doctor, then has responsibilities with special tools at their disposal. "Living well with lung disease is the personal responsibility of every patient who will accept it. We *can* do more for ourselves, physically, emotionally, spiritually. The only requirement is that we try.

"I love to help others. I love to see the spark of understanding and then the determination in patients. All most of them need is a little information and a nudge to get started. I get so much from being with the patients when I've been out talking with them, when the light bulb goes on, and they say, 'I can do this! I can do this!' The momentum has begun. It's got a life of its own."

Alpha-1 Antitrypsin Deficiency Facts

- Alpha-1 is one of the most common serious genetic conditions in America and is more common than Cystic Fibrosis.

- Alpha-1 can cause liver disease in children or severe liver and lung disease in adults, most often causing early emphysema.

- It is estimated that only 6,000 of the estimated 100,000 Americans with Alpha-1 have been diagnosed.

- An additional 24 million Americans are estimated to be genetic carriers of this disorder.

Since 1996 the World Health Organization has recommended that all individuals with COPD and adults and adolescents with asthma should also be tested for ATT Deficiency.

Source: Alpha-1 Foundation

Mary at 119 pounds, up 20 pounds from her low of 99.

Mary Pierce, Gold Medal Cyclist

Alpha-1 Quiz

- Are you age 20-50 and short of breath with little effort?

- Did you quit smoking with no improvement?

- Do you have frequent lung infections?

- Do you have asthma, emphysema, chronic bronchitis, or bronchiectasis?

- Do you have a family history of lung disease?

- Do you have cirrhosis and no history of alcohol?

You may have inherited A-1ATD. Please call for information and a confidential blood test. 1-877-2-CURE-A1

Embracing the Mission
John Walsh

In memory of Helen Chase Walsh

Arlington Massachusetts, a suburb of Cambridge, in the early 1950's.

In the Dutch Colonial home on Cheviot Street, life was very good. Robin Hood Road circled the neighborhood, with its sparkling lakes and beautiful woods, and Cheviot Street cut through the middle. There were about twenty families living in the valley. The families were more like family to each other than mere neighbors. Instead of the kids calling the parents of friends, "Mr. or Mrs. such and such..." it was more like "Uncle or Aunt." Fred Walsh, who lived there as a child, says simply, **"It was idyllic."**

Fred was one of four children, the younger—and quieter one—of twin boys, in the Walsh family. His mom, Helen, a former high school home economics teacher, was married to Jack, a popular high school football coach and college scout. The two had met years before while teaching at the same high school. Everybody loved Jack, gregarious, positive and generous. And everybody loved Helen.

95

Her other son, Fred's twin brother John, recalls, "Everybody could count on Helen to help with sewing the hem of a dress, or whatever. She'd help anybody. We kids could always bring friends home, and they would be welcome. It wasn't unusual for there to be twenty kids at our house for lunch. Whatever it was, mom was the 'go to' person—just an enormous strength. She was everybody's friend."

Fred, remembers, "She had a lovely singing voice. We would do supper dishes together and she'd sing, "The Isle of Capri."

Years earlier, already the mother of three-year-old Susan, Helen had a difficult pregnancy and didn't know until the last minute that she would give birth to twin boys, premature and fraternal. John and Fred Walsh were born in Boston on February 4, 1949. While she was still in the hospital Helen cleverly created hand-made birth announcements in a baseball theme, tied together with blue ribbons. They described Johnny and Freddy, as far as what "inning" they were born (time of day), and their "batting averages" (their weight).

It seems as if it would be a wonderful life for her, and it was; living in the beautiful Northeast countryside, having a loving husband, four bright and beautiful children, and adoring friends. But there was something very, very wrong with Helen Walsh. She couldn't breathe.

John says, "I think at first they thought it was asthma. She was on the original bronchodilators. You know, the little squeeze tube. We thought she had some lung disease, but they couldn't figure out why at such a young age and with such a healthy background, she'd be a sick as she was. We kids knew Mom was sick, but we had absolutely no idea how bad it was.

"She was a very proud woman. She didn't want us to know how badly she felt. Mom would build up the courage to be there for us when we got up for breakfast and get us out the door. We know now, it was after we left for school that the neighbors would come in. They would help out. Mom would rest as much as possible during the day and then make sure she had the energy to greet us and help us with our homework and everything when we came home. Then she'd divide up the chores. We all helped, but it was a while before we knew we had to help because she couldn't do it. I mean—helping—it was part of our family culture. It was a tradition we were brought up in—sacrifice and helping others.

"And then Saturdays when we were around, she always had a migraine headache. Freddy and I couldn't figure out why it was that during the week Mom would seem functional and on Saturdays she wasn't... And then on Sundays when we went to church, there would be a lot of reasons why she just wasn't able to come with us. And I mean, when we look back at it now, and that—being unable to function as a normal 30 or 40-something-year-old mom—that was her day *every* day."

Fred recalls, "I remember her being skinny, struggling, her nose was running all the time, but she never once complained. Never. Ever. But she was hiding something. She was hiding what she was going through each and every day. I think back now and realize that she never went up the stairs *with* me. She always went ahead or behind, because when she got to the top, she couldn't catch her breath."

John and Fred were just ten years old when their mother first went on oxygen. Their sisters, Susan and Judy, were ages 13 and 7. John says, "All I remember about it was that there was this green bottle and that she had to use it to help her breathe. Mom had frequent pneumonias and very difficult breathing on any exertion in the last few years. She had very limited mobility, and there was a point toward the end when she just stayed downstairs."

In spite of her sickness, Helen continued taking care of her family, using every ounce of energy to raise her kids and be there for whomever needed her. The Walsh kids were busily involved in scouting, school and church activities. John was president of his class and organized his friends in a small business doing odd jobs for neighbors.

John says, "Then Mom went into the hospital for the very last time. We had not internalized it. We just didn't have a clue she was that close. She never let us know just how sick she was. I mean, we knew she couldn't get out of bed, and she had the O_2 [oxygen] on. But we never thought she'd *die*.

"Mom was in the hospital. My grandpa, her father, died and we kids went to the funeral. My dad stayed at the hospital with mom. We came home from the funeral, and were walking up to the house, and saw that dad was on the front porch. We saw him—and we knew. *We just knew.* That was the first time I really understood what death was about."

Helen Chase Walsh died at age 46 as a direct result of complications from emphysema, leaving her husband Jack, daughter Susan, 16, twin boys, Johnny and Freddy, 13, and Judy, 10. She died in 1963, the same year her mysterious killer was identified at a medical research lab in Sweden. It was Alpha-1 Antitrypsin Deficiency.

Miami, Florida, November 2002

I was honored that John Walsh, co-founder, president and CEO of the Alpha-1 Foundation, and himself an Alpha-1 patient, had agreed to tell me the story of his life and his work. I was fortunate enough to have the opportunity to meet and interview him in his home city of Miami, Florida. Come along with me on my late November trip from snowy West Michigan to summer-like Miami. John and his wife, Diane are lovely people. Join us.

John very graciously met me at the Miami airport at 5:30 pm, just when his long workday should have been ending. My cell phone alerted me that a message was waiting. "Hi, Jane. It's John Walsh. I'll be waiting for you at United baggage claim."

I soon met John, a good-looking man, well dressed and appearing very healthy. As he lifted my luggage into the trunk of his car, I noticed the license plate—CURE A1. "It keeps me focused," he said.

Once in the car we immediately began to talk about the interview and his extraordinary story. "It's not about me. I don't want it to be about me. It shouldn't be. It's about the foundation and our mission: To find a cure for Alpha-1. And it's about the model we've created for other organizations."

John told me of his life as a boy and losing his mother to Alpha-1 some forty years ago when it was a nameless and perplexing disease. I met John's wife Diane, petite, pretty, and quiet but without a doubt tenacious, sharing with her husband the fierce determination to find a cure. I toured the Alpha-1 Foundation offices, painted in calming pale lavender, echoing the organization's trademark color. Travel-weary but feeling so privileged to have a part in sharing the Alpha-1 story, I joined John and Diane for an Italian dinner.

We met again the next morning, and over Cuban coffee talked for hours in John's office, which was quiet on that Saturday morning. I had with me a small tape recorder. "Is it OK if we test this first? To see if it picks up? You're kind of soft-spoken."

John laughed, "I don't know if anybody has ever accused me of being soft-spoken!"

But to my ear he was. His voice was quiet, calm, deliberate, determined. So determined. As John and I talked, Diane worked on Alpha information packets in her office down the hall. There, in the heart of the Alpha-1 Foundation, from the heart of its founder, I listened to the story of the man who knew the pain of loss, saw the need, heard the call, and quietly answered, "Yes."

~~~~~~~~~~~~~~~~~~~~~~~~~~~~~~~~~~~~~

What were your thoughts about what you wanted to do when you grew up? What were your ambitions?

"I was like any kid. I bounced from wanting to be a fireman to being an Indian chief. I was entrepreneurial. I always had a lawn mowing business and hired other kids in my class who would help mow lawns and paint houses. You know, clean up, fix up, paint up. And I always did the Boy Scout thing and sold Christmas wreaths."

You were organizing things back then, even at that young age?

He casually answered, "I seemed to have the natural ability to lead…to get things done.

"I really didn't want to go to college but if I had to go, I wanted to go to military college. So I went to Norwich in Northfield, Vermont. I wanted to make a military career. Once I got in I realized that it was not for me. Later I went to work in the Senate, for a ranking member of the Senate Oversight Intelligence Committee.

"Then I went to Saudi Arabia for 8 years and traveled extensively through the Middle East. I probably lived out my feeling that I wanted to do government service and to explore new areas, but that was a good personal challenge and good character building.

"I came back from Saudi in 1982 and by 1983 I began to be symptomatic. Freddy, my twin, born five minutes after me, was symptomatic at the same time. We were both diagnosed with allergy-induced asthma. I'd never had asthma before in my life. And back in Washington, the fall and spring and summer were killers, with the ragweed and the pollen."

So it was seasonal? Your breathing was worse at some times of the year, more than others?

John shook his head. "I never really thought about it. I just said, 'OK. This is asthma.' And I have to admit, even growing up I always thought, 'I don't want to suffer like Mom did. I don't want to have what she did.' And I mean, that's one reason why I never smoked. Every time somebody tried to hand me a cigarette, all I could think of was what I was putting into my lungs. There's *no way* I wanted to go there. So I just never smoked. Seeing Mom suffer like that—even though she never smoked. I drew the line and I just knew there was some connection there.

"But when we were diagnosed with asthma, for those five years, Freddy and I talked with each other. I

101

had a bout of pneumonia, he had a couple bouts of pneumonia. We were getting sick more frequently than we did before. It was obvious to us that our 'asthma' was really making us sicker than we thought asthma should. Freddy was really diligent about getting a more thorough diagnosis and pursued that."

In interviewing Freddy, at a later date, he told me, "I was something like 37 years old and working as a contractor. I was having trouble getting up the ladder. I would get a cold, and instead of lasting a few days, it would last for two weeks. I asked my family doctor *three times* over a couple of years, 'Is there a genetic emphysema?'

"'No,'" answered the doctor. "'What you have is allergenic asthma.'"

"But my mom died at 46 of emphysema, and my inhalers aren't doing what they used to do. Couldn't this be genetic?"

"'No.'"

"So I changed doctors and started going to somebody younger, a woman. She had me take a blood test and told me the results."

John continues. "So Freddy called me up, let's see, right around our 40th birthday and said, "I've got good news and bad news." Being the eternal optimist, I said, 'Give me the good news.'"

"He said, 'I know what we have. A genetic condition called Alpha-1 Antitrypsin Deficiency.'"

"I said, 'Alpha-what?' And he explained what it was—and that it was genetic."

And there it was.
"And here it comes," I thought. This is the part where he gets the news. This man sitting at the table across from me in this office in Miami, at this point in his story, at that moment in time, was just a man, a human being who was, along with his little brother, about to be handed a death sentence. He was not a successful businessman, foundation president and CEO, but simply one of thousands of people who knew what it was like to be thrust into a world of confusion and apparent hopelessness.

Although I knew what he was about to say, hearing him say it gave me chills. In a quiet, deliberate voice, John recounted more of the conversation he had had with Freddy. I could tell that the shock and the wounds left by the news he received 14 years ago still tugged at his heart, and now, at mine.

"And we were both silent for a minute and I said, 'I know what the bad news is.' We were both choked up and we said, 'Yeah, that's what Mom had.' And here we were at 40 years old. Mom died at 46. We kind of looked at each other over the phone and said to each other, 'There's just *no way* we want to progress as rapidly as Mom did, and there's *no way* we want our children to go through losing a parent.'

"Just then I thought of our lovely daughter, Linda, and how devastating it would be for her to lose her dad, just as I lost my mom... Then Freddy and I went on to say, '...and there's *no way* we want our children to have this.' I mean—it's genetic. The big deal is kids. It's families."

So what were your next thoughts?

"We made a commitment to each other right then that we were going to find out everything there was to know about Alpha-1, and we were going to do whatever we could to avoid the foreshortened life, and do whatever was necessary to figure out what we needed to do, health-wise.

At that time it wasn't an absolute, 'we're going to create a research foundation...we're going to do this and this and this.' But we did know we were going to find out everything we needed to know and do our part to make a difference.

"And the physician told him (Freddy) like the doctors told everybody then, 'You've got to get your affairs in order. You're going to have a greatly foreshortened life. You know your mom, you saw what happened with her. That's pretty typical. You're not going to be able to continue doing what you're doing. You're going to have to limit your physical activity.'

"I mean Freddy was physical, physical. You know, this [the thought of being so limited] was *frightening* to him.

"The doctor said, 'Look, there's a registry going on at the NIH (National Institutes of Health), they're doing a study.' The purpose of this seven-year study was to try to map out the pathogenesis and the natural history of the disease and figure out what the parameters were. 'You need to get your blood tested. You're fraternal twins, so it's not absolute, but there's a pretty good chance you both have it, based on the fact that you both have the same symptoms. So you ought to check it out.'"

"So I went over to NIH (I lived just a few miles from the institute right outside of Washington) and they actually drew my blood. Freddy came down and we joined the National Heart Lung and Blood Institute (NHLBI) longitudinal study, the NIH registry.

"We got there on the day that my results came back that I was also a homozygote (A homozygote is a person who has inherited two altered AAT genes, one from each parent). A person with these two "Z" genes is considered to have severe Alpha-1 Antitrypsin Deficiency."

How is Alpha-1 Inherited?

One half of your genes are inherited from each parent. Refer to the figure below to see the possible outcomes for children if both parents are carriers (having one normal and one altered AAT gene). This example applies to immediate family members, brothers and sisters only.

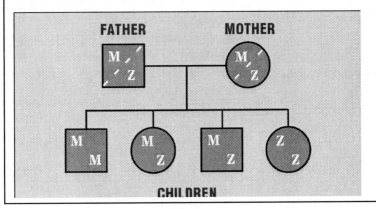

Source: Alpha-1 Foundation

Risks Associated with Common Genetic Variants

- **Normal (MM)** Does not have the disorder and does not carry any altered AAT genes.
- **Carrier (MZ)** Mild to moderate AAT Deficiency- may get disease symptoms and does carry an altered AAT gene.
- **Carrier (MS)** It is unclear whether there is a risk for getting disease symptoms but does carry an altered AAT gene (most studies do not show an increased risk for disease).
- **Alpha-1 (SZ) or (ZZ)** Moderate (SZ) to severe (ZZ) deficiency-could get disease and does carry two altered AAT genes.
- **Alpha-1 (SS)** It is unclear whether there is a risk for getting disease symptoms but does carry two altered AAT genes (most studies do not show an increased risk for disease).

Source: Alpha-1 Foundation

"I wasn't surprised. I just knew. And I thought, 'Thank God that our older sister Sue doesn't have symptoms.' And we were worried about my little sister because she smoked. At any rate, we arrived at the NIH with a bunch of questions. Freddy had a list that he and his wife, Pam, had developed. And I had a mental list.

"So we went in and asked, 'What's our life span?'"

"'We don't know,' they said.

"Should we move to Arizona or Florida?"

"'We don't know. There's no indication that it makes any difference.'"

"This was 1989, 26 years since Mom died and since they discovered Alpha-1! Freddy got frustrated and actually said, 'What's the oldest person you actually know with Alpha-1, *doctor?*'"

"'We really don't know...well...we... had someone who came in here last week who was 50.'"

"We asked about exercise. 'Well, there's some concern that with exercise you could enlarge the right side of your heart. We don't recommend specific exercise. But we really don't know. You have to be really careful. You shouldn't over exert.'" [It is now clear that exercise is very beneficial to people with Alpha-1.]

"It was very obvious to us then what they *didn't* know.

"When we left that first appointment at NIH, Freddy and I looked at each other and said, 'This is ridiculous. They really don't know a lot.' And it was very obvious to us that this was the *only* research going on for Alpha–1."

And you were thinking, "If they didn't know, who would?"

"Yeah, I mean this was the Mecca for health. I was surprised. We had so little information. We didn't know at first when we were diagnosed whether we'd go down to NIH and they'd give us a pill and we'd be all better, or what. I mean, *we really didn't know.* There wasn't any patient education information available. And that was one of many frustrations.

"The first frustration was, Mom died in 1963 when they knew Alpha-1 was identified in Sweden. My dad had the presence of mind when Mom died to say, 'Is this genetic? Is this familial?' And he's got a letter from that very hospital saying that it was *not* familial, or that they were not *aware* that it was familial. And then they came back a few years later and did a family study with my uncle and they didn't think to come to us, the offspring. I mean, why wouldn't you go the offspring of a woman that died of this disease that you suspected was familial because of her age and the symptoms?

"You know? That's inexcusable. There should have been something—a system in place to be able to tell the family members, 'You're potentially at risk here. You've got a genetic predisposition. It doesn't mean you're going to get the disease, but you know, you're at risk. Do you want to be tracked? Do you want to be tested?'"

"It's just inexcusable that family members don't have the option and the ability to make a decision as early as possible to be tested. And then they can make their lifestyle decisions, their career decisions, their family planning. There are just a lot of careers you wouldn't get into—because of the environmental risk factors—if you had a predisposition to developing this devastating lung disease. I mean that's the major motivation behind our focus of the screening and our mission statement. And it's 2002 and we're not there *yet*. We're making good progress, but we're not there.

"The second thing that got me really focused on creating the foundation was the experience at NIH and how important research was. Because I lived right up the street, every time they had a protocol relating to Alpha-1, I volunteered to go and participate in the research.

"The nurses started to call us when they got Alpha patients in. They'd call Diane and I up and say, 'Hey, we've got so-and-so from Hoboken, New Jersey here, or from Minneapolis, Minnesota. This person is really down. You want to stop by?'"

"And we'd stop down and we'd sneak them out for dinner at home and just chill them out and if somebody was feeling sorry for themselves we'd go and bring them down to the cancer ward or the ICU and see the kids who from birth were in trouble. And we'd say, 'Next time you start feeling sorry for yourself, just walk down the hall and think of that child. Imagine this being *your* child.'"

"And that was kind of like a virtual support group for people throughout the country. We met people from all over the country who came to the NIH for this study. And we were a source. And probably that's the way I began to deal with Alpha-1—to be connected with people who came in from out of town, and Diane and I would be help them. And consequently that's how I got involved with an organized effort for Alpha-1.

"At that time there were no formal educational materials to be found. I met somebody at a support group who had an idea for an educational CD Rom. It sounded like a great idea. So I raised $60,000. Susan Stanley, one of our co-founders was into computers. She found some college students who were able to develop a CD Rom – very, very elementary, compared to the technology today, but this was back in 1993.

"We were the only organization that we were aware of that created our own interactive educational program for newly diagnosed Alpha's. And we also created the Alpha Line. It gave people the access so they could call in and get a referral to a doctor in their area, or a support group in their area, or listen to information about Alpha –1.

"I had also realized the importance of connecting with other Alpha's to share mutual experiences. Ultimately we learn more from each other than from other sources. So we organized the Florida community. We had several support groups in Florida. We were the first chapter of the Alpha-1 Association. I tried to get involved on the patient side to organize. I was on the board of directors of the Association, which is located in Minneapolis, Minnesota and had a specific focus on support and advocacy.

~~~~~~

"In 1994 the NIH announced that the seven-year longitudinal study was going to stop. I was talking with a senior scientist [at that organization] one day and complained to him that the NIH was not as focused on Alpha-1 as they were on cystic fibrosis. And the response—the message from them—was very clear.

"The person I was talking to, a person in a key leadership position at NHBLI, was very direct and said, *'We've cured Alpha-1 with prolastin—with augmentation therapy. Unless you people get off your ass and do something, nothing's going to happen. We don't have the money or the interest. I mean, we're the government. We can't solve everybody's problems. Unless you organize the investigators, unless you organize the community, unless you raise money and work with us and put pressure on us to do the research, it's not gonna get done.'"

"And then I knew. I knew what I had to do. There was another researcher there named Mark Brantly. He basically said, 'John, there's nobody else that's going to take this on. This is your responsibility.' Flat out. It was very obvious to me at that time *this was not only what I had to do, but what I was here to do, and what still am here to do.*

"I said to myself, 'I know that I can do this.' So I spent several months, from February to October, looking at what other communities did for research, how they organized their research activities.

"In January 1995 we founded the Alpha-1 Foundation with Susan Stanley, a writer with a focus on internet stuff, and Sandy Lindsey who had experience with non-profits through the United Way. They were both Alpha's. In June of 1995 we founded AlphaNet. In October 1995 we expanded the board to include additional patients and people from the scientific and clinical community. It was officially stated that the majority of the board of directors had to be people with Alpha-1, so the decisions would always be stacked on what's best for the patient.

"We've got a unique organization. It's a true dynamic of the patients working with the physicians and scientists to make a difference for the future health of the people with Alpha-1 and COPD. And we've created an exceptional model for other organizations. We have the largest registry of both Alpha-1 and COPD."

Were there doubts about the scope of what you were trying to do? Did people say, "He's got this disease and now he thinks he's just going to go out and start a foundation..."

"Oh yeah, they thought I was whacked. We leveraged our property. It was a huge risk. Some of the criticism...it's taken its toll on Diane, and everybody. But we're doing the right thing. My dad always said, 'If you don't feel the arrows hitting your back, you're not leading.'"

And Diane is so involved.

111

"Diane is unbelievable. Clearly we wouldn't be where we are without Diane. She's a real unsung hero."

Was "no" ever an option?

"No" was never there. Instead it was, 'How are we going to juggle?' I had just invested in a business, moved to Florida, wanted to slow down and all the sudden I start this activity that jumps me right up to be as active as I ever was, work the hardest I ever have. The economic impact of that on Diane and me—I mean, we don't even think about it anymore."

You're a guy who watched his mom die and decided that you had no choice but to do your very best to fix it...would that be fair to say?

"No choice kind of sounds like it was, 'Tag, you're it'... And it was."

Did you think, "I can't not do it?" Otherwise you wouldn't be able to live with yourself?

"Yeah, that's the way I feel. Yeah, that's it. There's a reason I survived three surgeries. And they were tough surgeries. Everybody's had their near-death experience, but I've had a few. There was a tumor lodged in my spine twice, one mid-back, and one lower back. [To remove them involved] a very delicate surgical procedure. When I had my bypass my lung collapsed. They couldn't get it back up. The reason why I'm here today, the reason I never smoked a cigarette, the reason why I'm as healthy as I am, is because there needs to be somebody like me where I am, doing what I'm doing. And I think the combination of experiences I've had, the maturation process, has given me the ability to step up to the plate and do the job."

*It wasn't a question of **if**, it was a question of **how**?*

John paused and nodded. "Yeah, and we had to evaluate what was our best path. We've made some mistakes. But I look back at it—look at the time frame. We probably couldn't have built a registry any faster than we did. We could have funded the tissue bank, but we wouldn't have the Florida program to put it in. The stars were in alignment. I think what we've done has been very fast compared to the normal history of a voluntary health agency. It's been *lightning speed* compared to most orphan disease [an orphan disease is a disease affecting less than 200,000 people] community experiences. When you talk about the type of research we're doing and the progress that has been made in the last six years, it's mind-boggling. Now we need a bigger registry—the registry needs to grow, more research, more tissue samples. This all requires more resources, more money. We need more research."

"We've been very fortunate along the way...being able meet our co-founders, Susan and Sandy, for that dynamic to click where Susan was focused on that internet connectivity, knowing 'people are sick and they can't get out so let's create an environment for them on the internet to talk with each other in psycho-social support.' For Sandy, with her not-for-profit experience with United Way and American Heart Association being the ultimate conscience. Saying, 'John, you're an entrepreneur. You want to do it that way, but we really need process. Let's get the board involved and create a committee...' I was used to, well, not exactly being a one-man band, but I was used to charging on. That compatible, total synergistic fit was the magic. Then my entrepreneurial experience gave us the vehicle to run the engine and drive the boat.

Alpha-1 Foundation / AlphaNet

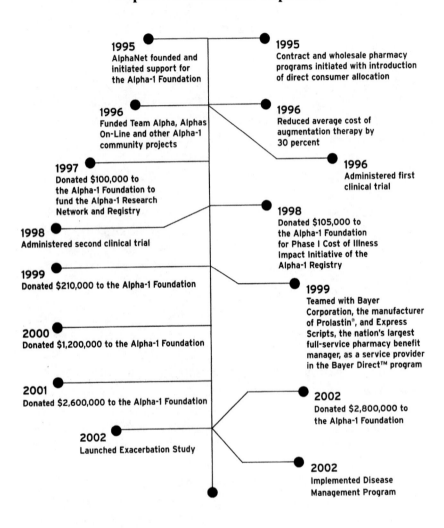

1995
AlphaNet founded and initiated support for the Alpha-1 Foundation

1995
Contract and wholesale pharmacy programs initiated with introduction of direct consumer allocation

1996
Funded Team Alpha, Alphas On-Line and other Alpha-1 community projects

1996
Reduced average cost of augmentation therapy by 30 percent

1996
Administered first clinical trial

1997
Donated $100,000 to the Alpha-1 Foundation to fund the Alpha-1 Research Network and Registry

1998
Administered second clinical trial

1998
Donated $105,000 to the Alpha-1 Foundation for Phase I Cost of Illness Impact Initiative of the Alpha-1 Registry

1999
Donated $210,000 to the Alpha-1 Foundation

1999
Teamed with Bayer Corporation, the manufacturer of Prolastin®, and Express Scripts, the nation's largest full-service pharmacy benefit manager, as a service provider in the Bayer Direct™ program

2000
Donated $1,200,000 to the Alpha-1 Foundation

2001
Donated $2,600,000 to the Alpha-1 Foundation

2002
Launched Exacerbation Study

2002
Donated $2,800,000 to the Alpha-1 Foundation

2002
Implemented Disease Management Program

Reprinted with permission of AlphaNet

"The dynamic of the Alpha-1 Foundation and AlphaNet, the combination of the two is very exciting. It's about helping individuals with Alpha-1, with AlphaNet providing both comprehensive care and the revenue to support research. We literally have created a model for other disease states. We've taken the time to talk with other organizations, sharing our documentation, whether it is policies and procedures for grants or registry formatting and software. We have given the template for our website to other organizations. *The importance is to share beyond our own community from our experiences so other people don't have to waste resources, as precious as they are.* They can invest in research and make a difference, not just duplicate what somebody else has already done."

So it just comes right back...

"The ultimate in recycling. The ultimate in recycling our insurance dollars—and what a good deal that is for society."

What is your everyday life like as far as your breathing goes?

"I've become more active. My mobility prior to my bypass in 1996 really slowed me down. After I had my bypass I breathed better. That's one thing with Alpha-1. We're so young, we don't have a lot of co-morbidities [other health problems], so every way you feel, you think its part of your lung disease. I had the angina [heart-related chest pain] for years and I nearly died from my heart when all along I thought it was my lungs. I thought at that time I was on a real fast progression with emphysema. But it ended up being mostly my heart. Then when I did Cardiac Rehab, rotating into a Pulmonary Rehab program I felt like a different person. Going through Pulmonary Rehab meant to me that I could have the ability to exercise without getting into trouble with symptoms.

"I've had a couple bad episodes though, from running in airports. Even today if I'm rushing to catch a flight, say a connection in Atlanta, or if I'm late to catch a flight, I can be in real trouble when I get to the gate. Even though everything I have is on wheels, sometimes I get to the gate and I can't even talk. I mean sometimes, you know, I forget, or disregard it. Then I focus on my pursed lip breathing. I tell myself, 'OK, I need this focus that I'm not gonna lose it.' And sometimes I have trouble lifting things.

"Talking and walking can be a problem. If I'm on Capitol Hill and walking with somebody and I'm going up the hill or in corridors and everything, the person I'm with can definitely tell I'm wiped out and winded. But otherwise, I don't think anybody can really tell. Sick lungs don't show. If I don't do my bronchodilators every day, I definitely have a tougher time than if I do them."

What do you take?
"Atrovent, Pulmicort, Ventolin."

Do you take prolastin?
"I do."

How long does it take?
"20 minutes to mix and 40 minutes to go in."

What about your family?

My older sister Susan is asymptomatic [without shortness of breath] at age 56, Freddie and I are 53. I'm around 41-42% [FEV1, the volume of air blown out in the first second of a lung function test]; he's now below 20%, on oxygen. He smoked for a few years, not a lot, and was exposed to an at-risk environment, being a teacher, then a contractor. All the dust and particulates, the machinery and stoves, you know, because he was up in Massachusetts. He should be out on disability, but he's busting his butt helping other Alpha's on AlphaNet. We have three of four siblings who we know now are homozygotes."

Do your siblings have children?

"Freddy has two daughters. Sue has a son and a daughter. And they're carriers. They have a higher predisposition to developing lung and liver disease than the average population. They're just not severely deficient. So do we have to worry about them? Absolutely. One of my nieces happens to have a neurological complication and the medication she takes torpedoes the liver. And she's got a compromised liver because she's a carrier. The ripple is pretty significant. Carriers are at a significantly increased risk of developing lung and liver disease. So it affects our kids."

How did the deaths of your co-founders affect you? Was that a stress on your own mortality? You're a very realistic person. You seem to see things in black and white.

"I had to do the eulogies. It was very difficult. Susan was more peripheral [in the organization] from day one. Sandy was very active for the first three years and then she got too sick to... I mean, she used to come to the office pulling her oxygen behind her [a tank on wheels] before they had the little oxy-lites [lightweight portable oxygen that can be carried]. I think there's no question they both lived longer than they would have, because they were as involved as they were. They had a real sense of accomplishment and pride at the progress we made. So that definitely helps as far as coping with loss. You know, part of their vision was clearly being realized, and when they died, part of their legacy to their grandchildren was in tact."

Are you saying that you feel they actually lived longer because of their involvement in the foundation?

"Oh yeah."

I'm sure that working around it gave them more useful information, of course. But do you think that just by the nature of them helping others, making a contribution, being of service to others—that prolonged their lives?

"No question in my mind and they did say the same thing. They had a better quality of life and they increased their longevity. They were engaged. They were helping their community. We've seen that over and over and over again. People who don't get involved, who are in denial or who are angry, *they die.*

"If you said that to a scientist, he'd say, 'Where's the data to prove that?' Answering his own question, John said, 'I think there is data. We've got some people who would love to use our coordinators in the study.

"There's absolutely no question in my mind, if you're actively involved in helping other people dealing with coping with the disease you have, you do better. You want to stay healthier longer because you know you're having an impact on somebody else. The more you're involved, the more you learn, the more you do pulmonary rehab, the more you do aggressive treatments of infections. If you need oxygen, you get on it sooner. Because you realize what happens if you don't go on oxygen.

"I'm not saying we live forever. I mean—we all die. I could get pneumonia this winter on a plane and die. But it's less likely."

Taking it one step further, do you think that involvement in that specific disease state helps the person to overcome more in that disease state? Say, more than being involved in another charitable, albeit, worthy cause?

"Absolutely. There's no question about it. There's absolutely no question in my mind.

"And there are pro's and con's. We have a coordinator in Pennsylvania who lost three Alpha's *in a week and a half. Three of her Alpha members died.* These are family members! The coordinators, Mary will tell you, and Shirley will tell you, and Joyce will tell you that the people who they coordinate services for, they're family. And [when you lose one of them] *it's brutal.* Part of our training for coordinators is grief counseling."

~~~~~~~~~~~~~~~~~~~~~~~~~~~~~~~~~~~~

Who inspired you? Was it the experience of losing your mother? Was that the catalyst for you?

"Realizing what Mom went through without even letting us *know.* Now I see hundreds of people with Alpha-1 at different stages of the disease, and now thinking of where my mom was. She was way down here, functionally (he motions with his hand below the table). And I would have thought she was up here (he holds his hand at face level). We kids talk about it to this day when we get together as a family. I mean, she was such a remarkable person with such courage and if she were here today she would be leading the charge. She would be very much involved with what we're doing now. If her generation knew then what we

119

know now, there's no question in my mind she would have grabbed the torch and dedicated her life to helping people with this disease.

"Mom exemplified the spirit of somebody who doesn't want to give up, who wants to have a good quality of life, who doesn't want anybody to feel sorry for them. She certainly didn't want us kids to know how sick she was, even at the very end. You know, it's not, 'The glass is half empty. The glass is half full.'

"And then there's my dad. He's always been a positive guy. He had to give up a very successful coaching career to take care of four kids. And he's everybody's favorite. He's everybody's friend. And dad's always been positive. We always lined up in the morning and said, *'Today I'm gonna be happy. Today I'm gonna be glad. Today's gonna be the best day I ever had'*—and walk out the door. It's always been that way. To this day, my dad is very involved. He is there at every Alpha event he can be. He's an amazing guy. So, clearly those two have been inspirations to me.

"Our Alpha doctors have had a tremendous impact. The Mark Brantlys and the Gordon Sniders, Jamie Stoller, Charlie Strange, Sandy Sandhaus, our medical director, to name just a few. Caring, committed, compassionate...*challenging*.

"Agusto Adorne, from 'Lorenzo's Oil.' You know, that was a message to me when I first saw that movie. Then I got the chance to meet him and I would have lunch with him occasionally. It was a tremendous inspiration that he would change his job. *He was a banker.* To think that he could later on do biochemistry along with the best of them. He had an impact on me saying, 'Well, wait a minute...you know, we can *do* this.'"

"*We have to do this.* I mean it's our responsibility. If we don't, nobody's going to do it. *And people are dying.*

"But the biggest inspiration I have of all is every time we lose somebody. Thinking back at Sandy Lindsey, just dragging herself into the office. Taking a half...three quarters of an hour...just to recuperate before she could even turn her computer on. How much more commitment and dedication can you have than that?

"And all along the way with the foundation it has been like the stars were in alignment. Ron Fraser, the famous coach, called me up one day. He said, 'Hey coach, I need to talk with you. My wife was just diagnosed [with Alpha-1].' And he was scared to death. The people from Mayo clinic and the NIH pointed them to us. We were the resource for them early on, giving his wife, Karen, an enormous amount of information. She's like a sponge. I mean, Karen is on top of it. That's one of the reasons why she's as healthy as she is. And she and Ron are very public, very social figures here in South Florida. And they made the decision to get involved. And the reason they made that decision is that this is a *responsibility*. It is a mission of people who have the disease."

So you inspired them?

"They were inspired by what we were doing. I hate to say I inspired them. Another person, Barbara Weintraub, just a wonderful soul. She knew Karen. And when Barbara met us she immediately said, 'Sign me up. What can I do to help?' This is wonderful. And they have provided funding for grants over the last few years, *at key times*. We got together with Barbara and we brought some other people around from the Cancer

Society and another local foundation just to brainstorm. And it was from that we set out as a mission to get the university program that was focused on Alpha-1 to be the support for the rest of the investigator community. We just really started to nail down the focus and set up an infrastructure to support the international investigative community. But that happened because Karen got involved, and then Barbara.

"Leo Fernandez and I met in Washington in 1972-73 as we were both getting out of the army. He later moved to Spain, established a business, sold it, and did very well. I'd kept in touch with his family over the years and when we formed the foundation, I was told that one of Leo's sons had Alpha-1 and was waiting for a transplant. We founded the Fernandez Family Liver Research Initiative. We get funding every year from the Fernandez family, supporting our liver research at a significant level. Marilina, Leo's wife, is an active member of our board of directors and Leo is very much involved with our strategic planning. *They came to us* because they recognized that we had the infrastructure to support research, and that we also had the international investigator community involved in our organization. They didn't do it because Leo and I met way back when, before I knew my mom died of Alpha-1, before he knew his mother was going to die of Alpha-1, before I knew that Freddy and Sue and I have Alpha-1, and before he knew he had two kids with Alpha-1. Talk about stars in alignment."

~~~~~~

What do you do for fun?

He laughed, and in seven hours of interviews that was the only question that John Walsh could not immediately answer. Even in the calm of his office, on a sunny Saturday morning, there didn't seem to be time for talk of leisure. Even in the interview, there was an immediacy, a need for him to do all he could to impart the information necessary to help people affected by Alpha-1.

How has this, heading the foundation, changed you?

"I've had to change from an entrepreneurial spirit to a consensus-building leader in a board—a group of dynamic, intellectually charged, and brilliant people. And here's little old me rallying the troops. Well, I've stepped up to the plate and done that.

"We have a total collegiate relationship and they don't expect me to act any differently than they do. We use that term, 'Partnering for a Cure.' It's that equal partnership between the medical and scientific community and the patient community that's made this organization succeed.

"I enjoy my work, and I enjoy the collegial interaction, and I enjoy the respect of the scientific leadership. I feel that the scientists embrace the fact that there are patients who can understand what they're saying and deliver the message. And they can embrace the fact that it has to be a true partnership."

John speaks of the scientific conferences sponsored by the foundation.

"We have patients at every thing we do. We always have patients there at the dinner table with all these brilliant minds from around the world. One of the constant comments is, 'It was so impressive that somebody affected by the disease was there to participate. It reminds me of what we're doing. It reminds me what we're all about.' It's one of the most exhilarating mechanisms I've ever seen. It's really exciting.

"It's just like with the Respiratory Therapist community. I mean, the Respiratory Therapists are people we should be using as our partners. Every one of our Alphas needs to be tagged with an RT. That needs to be a real mission. Mary [Mary Pierce, see page 77] founded and leads Team Alpha, getting people more involved by taking charge of their own care, and doing the physical exercise they are able to do, or helping somebody else do it. And that translates into disease management, into Pulmonary Rehab with the Respiratory Therapists inspiring somebody to be all they can be, and that's a critical component. We need a partnership with professionals who understand the physiology and the other aspects of Alpha-1."

~~~~~~

I asked him again. "What do you do for fun?"

"I swim at night."

Do you have any hobbies... or is this your life?

"No...this is what I do. I can't think of doing anything more meaningful."

You had mentioned that Diane and you had said, "We're going to move to Miami now [when you were in your forties], we're not going to wait until we're old. We're going to go now and enjoy it." I think more people should do that. But especially you, with a chronic—

"But, even without! Life is life! You could die before me. You need to live life and you need to live it to its fullest and I think you need to live it responsibly. What you're doing, writing this book, this is going to inspire a lot of people. You didn't need to do that, but you did it. And that's the way I feel about what we're doing. Is this what I intended to do at this time in my life? Is it what I expected? No way."

John points to his desk. "That's why Mom's picture is right there. There's no question in my mind that there's a message from those Alpha Angels, we call them, the people who have died who had Alpha-1. The message is, 'Don't let this happen over and over and over again.' We made a commitment to Sandy and Susan and we all made commitments to each other that we weren't going to let anything get in our way to accomplish our mission: *To provide the leadership and resources to increase research, improve health, promote world-wide detection and effect a cure.*

"I had to do... [he murmurs] one, two...five or six eulogies this year. I couldn't say no to the families. Every one of them [every death from Alpha-1] makes me further resolved to push the envelope to make this happen. And I think anyone involved feels the same way. Every time we lose somebody when they are in the ER [and they receive inappropriate treatment] because they [the staff] didn't realize how deteriorated the patient's lungs were, we all shake our heads and say, 'There's no excuse for that in 2002.' It happens over and over and over again. We've got to change the way people with Alpha-1 are treated and we've—we've got to have a cure. We've got to have therapeutic solutions. And close to it—right there—is a cure.

"If we don't do it, nobody else will. It's our responsibility and if we don't do it, shame on us. It's for our children and grandchildren. It's not for our generation. This whole generation's getting wiped out. The last three, four years have been brutal and it's gonna get worse. But that's the reality. That makes it our generation's responsibility to create the vehicle for a cure. The reality is that we started, we created the momentum, and this has been done because the community has taken responsibility and taken charge. They've rolled their sleeves up and done it, and are doing it. And I really feel confident we're going to have some definite solutions in this decade."

So that's your biggest hope. To find a cure within this decade?

"Yes."

"The doctors used to argue about using the 'C' word. 'It's dangerous. There are false hopes,' they said. If cure is a therapeutic pathway, a solution for prevention of symptoms and progression of the disease, maybe that's it. But the *ultimate* cure is to eradicate it. The ultimate cure is to put a gene in so it is not passed on to the next generation. The vision is to eradicate the disease.

"When Sandy Lindsey died, one of the last times I saw her she said, 'John, you've got to slow down and force yourself and the organization to tell the story.'

"And I'm deliberately doing that now. Now we've got the infrastructure, we're supporting an enormous amount of research compared to what other organizations are doing and we've got to tell the community what we're about and what we're doing. We've got publications going out every six months or so to let people know what's going on.

"And everyone who is in the registry gets updated every six months. That was based on our experience from the NIH. Back then we didn't get any information. *We never got any information for 6 years!* We schlepped to different institutes around the country to do this research project and that, and never got any information. We made our commitment when we formed our registry to say, 'You are going to be given information about what research is going on and about results from your participation.'

"Right now we're planning a public awareness program. Once people realize that 25 million people are affected by this, I mean, that's 10% of the population. It's *huge*. More awareness. That's the ripple. More people could care. More people might contribute. More ideas might emanate. You know, the mentality is—we're in a rush. *We can't let another person die.*"

So there's a real sense of urgency.

"Yes, there's an absolute sense of urgency. Up to this point we've been focused on the end target. We've got to backfill now and bring more people along. Because—it's everybody. We're of the community. The majority of our board is Alpha-1. This is not a singular effort. We're part of a proactive community taking responsibility, taking charge, creating the infrastructure to support research which is going to end up with a cure for this disease, and perhaps facilitate the cure for other diseases as well."

It's a contagious energy. I can feel it. I'm hearing everybody saying, "We've got to fix this."

"This is an amazing community of really dedicated people. The AlphaNet coordinators – they are true heroes. The board, the scientific leadership, the supporters, the staff. All of them. We've got people who have gotten involved and helped us get to the next level each and every time. They embrace the mission. They feel empowered. That's the message. You have to take responsibility for your own health and then stay involved to help others."

Note: In the last 20 days of the year 2002, since this interview took place, eleven members of AlphaNet died.

Helen Chase Walsh, circa 1940's

John is honored with the "Distinguished Achievement Award" for outstanding contributions to humanity, the medical profession and the University of Florida, May 2001.

The Walsh Family
Diane, John, Linda and Christian Dopp
Don and Sue Ferro, Fred, Jack
(sister Judy, not pictured, was unable to attend)

Alpha-1 Resources

www.alphaone.org
Alpha-1 Foundation 1-877-2-CURE-A1

www.alphaoneregistry.org The Alpha-1 Research Registry 1-877-886-2383 Alpha-1 carriers are encouraged to join this confidential research registry.

www.alphanet.org A not-for-profit disease management company 1-800-577-ANET

www.alpha1.org Alpha-1 Association 1-800-521-3025

www.liverfoundation.org American Liver Foundation 1-800-GO-LIVER

Section Five

Interstitial Lung Disease
Pulmonary Fibrosis

*"Maintain a good sense of humor and enjoy life to the
fullest extent you possibly can.
What is life if you can't contribute that much?"*
Lois Felinski, Warren, MI

Memory Treasures to Store

Dale

"Never give up.
God wants us to do the best we can with what we have."
Justin Johnson, Holland, MI

Dale Van Langevelde's smile lit up the room. He was a tall man with sparkling eyes, a happy face and thick, silvery white hair. I knew him only when he was on prednisone, so in spite of his failing health he always looked robust, tanned, and full-faced. While exercising in rehab the report of a low oxygen saturation was usually met by him with a smile and a sense of humor. What else could we do in rehab but try to keep his muscles strong and his spirits up? Dale was a sharp dresser, casual but crisp, always coming to class wearing a nice pants and shirt. He worked hard at exercise, even though he was very short of breath and in spite of transtracheal oxygen at 4-6 liters per minute, maintained oxygen saturations in the low to mid 80's.

This is the story of Dale who had Pulmonary Fibrosis, as told by his wife, Mary.

"First, after diagnosis, came the many questions—but wanting only the answers we want to hear. Then came the time frame—how long can he (we) be active, how will this progress, how will his last days be, and what kind of death can he expect?

"Some of these can be answered by qualified personnel, others can only be answered as time progresses, some only when we meet our God face to face.

"Dale often remarked what a cruel disease this was—yet our days together became very special—a new interdependence, with myself the 'strong' one. How I played the 'strong' role, wanting to give Dale the peace of mind he so pursued. My tears were inward, private, or suppressed—showing only when a tender moment or happening occurred.

"We learned more about oxygen tanks, ice crystals, and frozen parts that we thought we ever needed to know. But we handled all these 'crises' only to learn a lesson for the next time.

"One night (before full time oxygen) we returned from bowling with friends when Dale felt he needed some additional air. Our friends wondered what was so important that he needed to use the phone. (This is what they thought he was doing!)

"Nineteen ninety-six was the year of our 45th wedding anniversary. Our children offered to give us an open house if we wanted. Thinking it might not be possible in another year (is this ESP, or what?) we agreed. Dale had been active in singing in a barbershop chorus and quartets for over 30 years. Of course the men in his quartet were invited and he and his group sang songs all evening - even as he received oxygen through his transtracheal catheter. Many of those songs were the 'old timey' ones - some were love songs sung especially to me. This was June 8, 1996 - I had no idea that his life would be over on July 18 of that year. Saturday, July 13, he still sang the barber-shop tunes he so loved - even though he had to sneak extra breaths!

"Whatever choices were left to us, after losing much of his mobility, we chose to do as much as possible. Not always a conscious decision—but one we had always embraced—do it, see it, as much of life as we could encompass.

"Our choice was to take a family vacation, a cruise. On June 20 Dale, our daughter Karen, and I started out on the drive to Miami, Florida. We took with us our 100-gallon oxygen tank, two portable tanks, water, towels, basin (for the inevitable freeze-up of the oxygen ports), not to mention suitcases, coolers, and all the usual paraphernalia needed for a long trip. On Sunday the 23rd we were to board a ship with two couples of our three children to cruise for a week.

"Much of Dale's time on the cruise was spent in be-ing chauffeured (in a wheelchair) by various family members. Each was jealous of his turn to chauffeur Dad. Sitting out on deck usually turned into naptime, but Dale always woke up in time to go to the casino and with plenty of quarters in hand, have his chair adjusted in front of a 'hot' slot machine. He was as delighted as a little kid when he would win $10.00— even though it had cost him twenty or so to win.

"After all the hard work on that trip, loading and unloading all the paraphernalia, wheeling Dale into men's bathrooms (hoping they weren't already occu-pied), dealing with all the inconvenience of handi-capped travel—it was worth it only to hear Dale say, *'I'm so glad we went. I had such a good time!'* Reward enough! We now had memory treasures to store up for a time when only memories would be left.

"Returning from our trip July 1—to see a rapid descent of health. How could we give up more? There was so little left! The anxiety attacks never seemed to leave him, and the dependency on myself and others grew. Rides in his wheelchair were given even though he protested—'I don't know how long I can do this,' and ended in wanting to be left out in the sun and warm breezes.

"Hospice had been summoned and we faced the certainty of imminent death. How can we face a final parting? Partners for 45 years - now partners no more - not imaginable!

"Those final moments of our life together began when I called our Hospice nurse to help me get Dale out of the wheelchair and back into the hospital bed. He wanted the head of the bed made level (he hadn't slept on a level surface for some time) and when he was put into this bed he breathed irregularly for a few breaths—and my love, my lover, and my friend found his sought-after peace. I was able to say good-bye and assure him of my love, and he left me for a distress-free, celestial place.

"My words of wisdom after my experiences with disease, dying and death would be:

- Love each other as unconditionally as humanly possible.
- Tell each other of your love and appreciation.
- Live your lives as fully as your physical condition will allow.
- Let other loved ones support and care for you both."

Do not stand by my grave and weep
I am not there... I do not sleep.
I am a thousand winds that blow
I am a diamond glint on snow.
I am the sunlight on ripened grain
I am the gentle autumn rain.
When you awaken in the morning's hush
I am the swift uplifting rush
Of quiet birds circling in flight
I am the soft star shine at night.
Do not stand by my grave and cry
I am not there, I did not die.

Anonymous
Submitted by Mary Van Langevelde

Mary and Dale Van Langevelde on the cruise

Feeling Blessed

Marilou

"Attend classes, exercise (can't stress that enough),
talk with people who have the same disease."
Edwin Brubaker, Sterling Heights, MI

A retired librarian and teacher, Marilou Parker has taken charge of her health by researching her disease, following a good management plan, and helping others. She participates in a pulmonary rehab maintenance exercise class, always ready to offer a classmate a word of encouragement or a listening ear. Quiet and gentle, but very determined, she identifies with others, empathizes in difficult times, and rejoices in success. Here, in her words, Marilou tells of her life with asthma and pulmonary fibrosis.

The hayloft with its many large bales of hay was an exciting and fun place to play *hide and seek*, especially at night. But suddenly, something was wrong. I could not breathe. My playmates helped me down the stairs and across the lawn to the house where my mother was visiting our neighbors. Mom and I sat

137

outside on the step by the back door. The air was chilly. The sky was filled with thousands of stars. Mom gently rubbed my back, comforting me, while the cool air cleansed my lungs of the dusty hay. I was three years old. This is my first memory.

The years went by, filled with similar episodes of asthma, colds, pneumonia, whooping cough, pleurisy, and bronchitis. Not always being able to easily breathe was part of growing up. Many nights I struggled to breathe, finally falling asleep sitting up in bed. Back in the forties, fifties, and sixties, no breathing medicines were available for "rescue," let alone control and avoidance of breathing problems. All I could do was "tough it out." Over time, these episodes of infection and inflammation took a toll.

Five years ago my 80-year-old brother died of pulmonary fibrosis, with no cause being determined for the scarring of his lungs. I was familiar with the symptoms of shortness of breath and a dry cough. My sisters, both heavy smokers in the past, suffer with COPD (Chronic Obstructive Pulmonary Disease). Three years ago I, too, was diagnosed with pulmonary fibrosis.

After being diagnosed I researched the disease on the internet. The American Lung Association (ALA) website (www.lungusa.org) was the most informative and easiest to understand. At the home page I clicked on "Diseases A-Z," and then "P" for Pulmonary Fibrosis and Interstitial Lung Disease from the disease list. According to the American Lung Association:

Pulmonary Fibrosis is also called Interstitial Lung Disease (ILD), which is a general term that includes a variety of chronic lung disorders. When a person has ILD, the lung is af-

fected in three ways: First, the lung tissue is damaged in some known or unknown way. Second, the walls of the air sacs in the lungs become inflamed. Finally, scarring (or fibrosis) begins in the interstitium (or tissue between the air sacs), and the lung becomes stiff...Fibrosis, or scarring of the lung tissue, results in permanent loss of that tissue's ability to transport oxygen. The level of disability a person experiences depends on the amount of scarring of the tissue. This is because the air sacs, as well as the lung tissue between and surrounding the air sacs, and the lung capillaries are destroyed by the formation of scar tissue...

The American Lung Association goes on to state, "The diseases may run a gradual course or a rapid course. People with ILD may notice variations in symptoms... from very mild to moderate to very severe. Their condition may remain the same for long periods of time or it may change quickly." I find it very encouraging that the disease may progress gradually.

The ALA website also discusses treatment and management for my disease, idiopathic (unknown cause) pulmonary fibrosis (IPF). One important component of management for me is to reduce episodes of inflammation and infection. I have a pneumonia vaccine when appropriate, as well as an influenza shot each fall. These two shots help prevent infection.

The ALA suggests that rehabilitation and education programs may help some people with IPF. I joined the Pulmonary Rehabilitation class at our local hospital. The staff taught me how to breathe under stress, encouraged me to do tasks more slowly, and to take more frequent rests. For example, I learned how to vacuum the carpeting without becoming impatient and frustrated with my limitations. I could do it; I just had to vacuum a smaller area and rest for a few minutes or wait until the next day to complete the job.

The exercise during rehab class has sometimes been a challenge, but always a benefit. I have been able to increase my time and speed on the recumbent stepper and the treadmill during the past two years. Though the staff is right there to advise me, the goals I've achieved are not necessarily set by them. I am motivated to set my own goals and to improve my exercise duration. This helps my self-esteem. I know now that *I can improve!*

Since the therapists or nurses check our lungs twice a week before class, they hear the subtlety of our crackles, wheezes, squeaks and whistles. They discern changes. A staff member may remind us to be more diligent in taking our medicines or may suggest that a visit to the doctor is in order. Each fall the pneumonia and flu vaccines are available to us during class time. I am helped by the constancy and compassion of these health care professionals who specialize in respiratory care and offer us their expertise and encouragement.

Another significant component of the rehab class is classmate support. We are attuned to one another's breathing problems. We care deeply when another person is having a bad day. We encourage each other with the thought that maybe tomorrow the weather will be better and it will be easier to breathe. (In Michigan the weather is blamed for everything!) While working out on the treadmill, I often look around the room and observe my friends. I admire their tenacity, their spirit.

Sixty-two years have passed since I played *hide and seek* in the neighbor's hayloft. The many changes in health care since that time are significant. New medicines are available for breathing problems, ongoing research offers possibilities of cures, and medical professionals and rehabilitation offer support. Do I hope for a cure? Sure, I do! Meanwhile though, I continue with the daily management and treatment of my pulmonary fibrosis and asthma, waking thankfully each morning for a good night's sleep and feeling blessed.

Jackie

Jackie Glass was a ray of sunshine in our Pulmonary Rehab class. Even though she has scleroderma (a restrictive disorder involving the connective tissue in the lungs) among other illnesses, Jackie glows with a positive attitude and strives to be of help to others. Whether it was a ride to rehab or simply a word of encouragement needed, Jackie was always there. She is often heard saying, "Each day holds new promise." Here are two of her poems.

Jackie Glass on vacation in the Bahamas

Joy

Joy comes on the wings
Of a fresh morning dew.
Joy comes in the cacophony
Of sweet bird songs
Filling the morning stillness.

Joy comes brand new and powerful
As I observe a glorious sunrise -
Parting the veils at dawn's demise!
Joy comes brand new and powerful!
More awesome because of limits.
Special, special, special!

I choose joy above the limits.
I know of labored breathing
I know of limited activity,
Of foreign fingers that grip my lungs.
Yet - joy springs up daily.

One joyful and sincere smile -
Is worth a thousand words!

© Jackie Glass
September 5, 1999

143

A Merry Heart

I'm so pleased to meet you.
Your smile is special to me.
Your handshake fills me with
Encouragement!

I greet you with a merry heart.
See the joy on my face,
The shine in my eyes,
The smile on my lips!

I may be limited by chronic breathing problems,
but I still have limitless vision.
I have a keen sense of smell,
And my hearing is just fine!

My mind is full of ideas!
For good vision, for good smell,
And good hearing, thankfulness
Pours out with ever beat of my heart!

Chronic breathing problems
Cannot change my merry heart.
I choose to enjoy all things, you see.

Your smile, your touch
Your merry heart;
Feel like victory to me!
You have made my day!

© Jackie Glass
September 5, 1999

144

Interstitial Lung Disease and Pulmonary Fibrosis Facts

Interstitial Lung Disease (ILD) includes a variety of chronic lung disorders. When a person has ILD, the lung is affected in three ways:

- Lung tissue is damaged in some known or unknown way

- The walls of the air sacs in the lungs become inflamed

- Scarring (fibrosis) occurs in the tissue between the air sacs and the lungs become stiff

Breathlessness with exertion and a dry cough are common symptoms that many people ignore until they feel quite ill. It is important to see your doctor when symptoms begin, to stay in touch with your doctor and report any changes.

The course of these diseases is unpredictable, running a gradual or rapid course. Pulmonary Fibrosis may be caused by:

- Exposure to inorganic dusts (e.g., asbestos fibers) or organic dusts (e.g., mold, fungi)

- Chemotherapy or radiation therapy

- Lung infection

- Connective tissue disease such as scleroderma or rheumatoid arthritis

Keep Breathing

John

I met John Widmayer on a cold and snowy day in January, 2003. He had driven alone, 30 miles from his home in Howard City, Michigan, to meet me at a German restaurant in Grand Rapids. His pulmonary rehab nurse, Mary Ann, had told me of John's significant progress in increasing his six-minute walking distance from a mere <u>54 feet</u>, to nearly ten times that—and thus, qualifying for placement on a lung transplant list.

"What kind of person is that?" I wondered, who has the courage—the plain old guts—to travel 30 miles (his sister drove him at first) to exercise when he can barely walk the width of a narrow city lot?

So I met John, age 49, who was waiting for me as I entered the restaurant ten minutes earlier than our appointed time. He sat on a bench in the foyer, wearing an oxygen cannula attached to a small tank. Hanging around his neck was a small personal use oximeter, a device used to make quick oxygen level checks.

I found John to be quiet, soft-spoken, shy. We were told by the hostess that our table was ready. John stood slowly, then methodically turned the bigger tank on, switched his nasal cannula to that tank, increased the liter flow, turned the small tank off, and turned to follow the hostess. Although we had to walk only about 40 feet to get to our table, John needed the increased oxygen flow for that increased physical workload. We ordered lunch and after some get-acquainted small talk, began to speak about his life and his work. John had a lot to say. He had been through a lot, learned a lot, and knew himself well. I was impressed with his kindness, his strength, his courage.

What did you do for a living?

"I worked as a die-caster in an injection molding plant for 26 years. We sprayed acids. Sometimes you couldn't see to the other end the plant, the air was so filled with smoke."

Did you wear a mask?

"No, we didn't think anything of it then. And I smoked while I worked."

My mouth dropped open. I looked at John straight on, as if to say, "You've got to be kidding." He knew exactly what I was thinking, shook his head, and smiled a knowing smile.

"I know. I'd smoke four to five cigarettes an hour. In an eight-hour day, that made about 40 cigarettes – two packs. It kept me going."

We went on to talk about conditions in the plant, how bad they were, and how the air quality has improved in more recent years.

"The 'Right to Know' Act[3] helped. After that was passed, they improved the ventilation."

But for you, it was too little, too late?

"Yep. Then I got the diagnosis – Pulmonary Fibrosis. I'd never heard of that before."

What about wearing oxygen? Were you ever afraid to go out with it? Concerned what people would think?

"No, I didn't care what they thought. I'd seen people with it, and they needed it. I needed it for a reason. Now people see it and they ask, 'Do you have emphysema or asthma?' I tell them I have Pulmonary Fibrosis and explain that it is caused by the way my lungs react to a certain chemical. It does take some getting used to, though. You know, you're in the grocery store and you see something over there, and go to get it. He smiles again, a little smile and says, "And your oxygen is way back there… in the cart."

What is your life like today?

"Well, I live with my sister and her family. I do what I can if I feel up to it. The other day I was having a really good day and I scraped the snow off my van. I'm single, so that [the oxygen] makes it a little more lonely."

So, the girls aren't lining up to date you, is that what you mean?

He smiles and shakes his head, "No."

"Sometimes I get depressed. It's hard, especially in the winter. But I just can't let the depression get me down. I try to keep active. I visit with somebody or watch a video. Going to rehab helps."

148

Following are some suggestions from John—things to do and things not to do. This is wisdom for all of us, from a man who has been down—way down—and fought his way back to better health and a hopeful future.

Knowing what you know now, some four years after your initial diagnosis, what do you wish you had known then, when you were first diagnosed? In other words, if a person came to you today and said, "John, I just found out I have Pulmonary Fibrosis. Help! What can you tell me? What do I need to know?"

- Make sure you have a good pulmonologist [lung doctor], one who has up-to-date information on pulmonary fibrosis and treatment programs.
- Have him [or her] enroll you into a Pulmonary Rehabilitation program with education and exercise.
- Make sure your family doctor understands pulmonary fibrosis and any special needs you might have.
- Have the pulmonologist start the process of testing and evaluation for getting you on a lung transplant list.

What are the three most important things, the three best things, somebody can say to a person with Pulmonary Fibrosis?

- We are praying for you.
- Don't give up.
- They can me questions about the disease.

Those are words of wisdom from a man who knows.
Now, finally, here is John's list of things <u>not</u> to do.

- Don't smoke.
- Don't go without your oxygen.
- Don't forget to pace yourself.
- Don't forget to pursed-lip breathe.
- Don't sit around and do nothing—try to get out whenever possible.
- Don't expose yourself to illnesses, such as colds or flu, when possible.
- **Don't give up!**

John Widmayer

Miracles

Leslie

"I've got strong shoulders. I figured God chose me to go through this. Whenever something bad happens, I figure he must have found another empty spot on my shoulders."
Linda Blevins, Logan, West Virginia

Being from the agricultural and industrial Midwest, I was somewhat unfamiliar with Black Lung and other pulmonary diseases caused by mining. My author's advocate from Infinity Publishing in Pennsylvania is John F. Harnish. As a child, John's life had been deeply touched by loss from Black Lung, and he encouraged me to include a story and information on this disease.

In my search I learned of Leslie Blevins, a miner with silicosis. I read about him and was quite sure, as the account seems to indicate, that it wouldn't be long after the newspaper telling his story went to print in 1998 that Leslie would have lost his battle with this cruel disease. There was, however, another – perhaps a divine – plan.

In order to complete my research in early 2003, I needed to talk with Linda Blevins. I thought surely that Les had died and I wanted to speak with his wife, Linda, about her memories. Calling directory assistance and asking for a listing in Logan, West Virginia, I had no idea first of all, if there would be such a listing, and if there were, if I would get the number, or even then, if Linda would honor my request.

There was indeed a listing for a "L. Blevins" in Logan. I called and left a message explaining who I was and asked Linda to please call just to let me know she got the message, whether or not she wished to talk. About two hours later my phone rang.
"Hello?"
"A throaty voice with a slow Southern drawl, said, "This is Blevins."
"Oh...yes... is this Linda?"
"This is Les." His inflection slowly swept upward, making the name 'Les' into two syllables.
I was stunned -- completely stopped in my tracks, as if I were talking to a ghost. "Oh... well... how are you?"
"Doing fine."

Here is the story of Leslie Blevins' battle with silicosis, his wife Linda's faith, and their astounding victory.

Leslie Blevins has been breaking barriers all his life. The second son of 12 children from a family of hard-working miners, Les grew up in the Pine Creek coal camp just outside Logan, West Virginia. Following the noble family tradition he labored underground for over 21 years. He took pride in providing for his family as a miner, breaking through the natural barriers of this rocky earth to bring forth the fuel, the energy, that is coal. His livelihood would earn him a decent living indeed, but tragically as well, what would seem to be a swift and early death from the most virulent form of Black Lung Disease.

"Working the mines is something I always wanted to do," Les said. "My dad worked in the mines, Grandpa worked in the mines." He says slowly, reconciled to the limitations of Appalachian opportunity, "It's what there was."

In August of 1969 Leslie and his brother, Virgil, joined the Army. Three years later his enlistment was up, he came home to Logan, and married Linda. After a frustrating year of working odd jobs, Les was hired to work a three-foot seam of coal in a union mine. Doing this was something like crawling under a kitchen table and spending the day shoveling from a stooped over position. At the end of the first day, Les was so sore from crawling and stooping he couldn't stand upright. He barely made it home—crawling all the way. He was 23. But the next day, he was back in the mine again. Leslie remembers, "On my fourth day there I was, down on my knees, shoveling, when the earth rumbled and the roof fell in. It broke my left foot and the toes on my right foot." When his broken bones had healed he was back in the mine. He boldly said, "I'd go back today if I could. I loved the work that much."

In 1993 the union mine closed. Leslie was out of work for about six months before being hired to work as a mining-machine operator at a nearby non-union mine operated by RMI Contracting. He could finally work standing up because his job at that time was working a seam of coal that was 7 feet high. However, his pay dropped from $16.92 an hour to only $11.25. Although this was one of the most dangerous jobs in America, the important thing to Les was that he was supporting his family with a job he loved doing.

After mining the seam of black rock for just about a month, he hit a wall of sandstone. His bosses told him to cut through the sandstone to get to coal that had to be there. "They cleared everybody out of the area where I was doing the cutting because they said they wanted them doing other things," he said, "But I know now the real reason was they knew how dangerous the dust from working the sandstone is if you breathe it."

Linda recalls, "I remember it. He'd come home all covered in white dust—totally exhausted and completely drained. He'd get in his chair and fall fast asleep in minutes. I'd have to wake him up to feed him dinner. Then he'd go right back to sleep for the rest of the night. In the morning, he'd leave for another day of trying to work through the sandstone to find the coal."

When Les started cutting through the sandstone, he was using a relatively new mining machine operated by a remote control that enabled him to stand out of the way of some of the dust. Les said, "You know, sandstone is much harder than coal, and the work of cutting through it was tearing the machine apart. So the owners decided to make a profit while they still could, and they sold the mining machine. They took a much older machine out of the shop for me to work the sandstone with. This one didn't have no remote, so I was forced to sit on the machine in the middle of all the dust the machine was making. At times the machine would shake so violently that it would toss me up against the ceiling of the mineshaft. Another thing was, the water sprayers that were supposed to wet down the dust were always breaking down. They were worthless. The dust was so suffocating that sometimes I'd have to shut down the miner [the machine], go back into the fresh air and just puke. Then my boss would come by and tell me to go back in and keep working."

Les spent over three months grinding sandstone to get to the coal. "I knew I'd pay the price for breathing in all that dust," Blevins said, "I just didn't think it'd happen so quick."

The menacing threat of silicosis—the world's oldest known occupational disease—was known to the Greeks even in ancient times. Leslie knew the sandstone rock dust was particularly unhealthy, but he explained, "There's a whole lot of things that wasn't supposed to be done like it was being done then, but you either did it as you were told to, or you lost your job and went home."

OSHA requires mine operators to test the air in the mines every two months. This is done to make sure the dust levels don't exceed the federal limits. Les said, "I never took a dust test while working on cutting through the sandstone. I don't recall a proper dust sample being taken during the entire two years I worked at RMI."

According to OSHA records, RMI took 12 dust samples during the three months Les was cutting through the sandstone. The test samples were supposed to be taken where the mining machine operators were working. However, nine of the tests indicated a measurement of just 0.1 mg. of dust per cubic meter of air—the readings so unusually clean that the federal experts figured they must be inaccurate. Tests supervised by government mine inspectors during 1991 through 1993 showed far higher amounts of silica dust. As a result of these tests, RMI was cited four times in those years of operation for exceeding federal dust limits and fined a total of $1,681.

In order to keep his job, Les was expected to help conceal unsafe practices from the federal mine safety inspectors. "Whenever a mine inspector showed up, the bosses would tell me to quit cutting away the sandstone, shut off the power to my work area and go some place else to work in the mine," Blevins confided. "I didn't complain because I had a job to do."

Reminded of the dangers of mining, things he had seen and experienced, even the devastating lung disease members of his own family had known, Les was asked if he ever thought about just getting out. His answer was, "This is what we do. When I was growing up that's all I looked forward to. It's just bred into a person."

~~~~~~~~~~~~~~~~~~~~~~~~~~~~~~~~~~~~

Les said that he first noticed he was having breathing problems in 1990. "Getting short of breath is natural for a coal miner." He says quietly and matter-of-factly, "That's part of coal mining. Anyway, in 1994, I went to the doctor because my breathing was so bad. The workman's comp doctor told me I had cancer. That hit hard. So I went back to my family doctor and he did biopsies and other tests, and they said it was silicosis. They did more tests, you know, to rule everything else out. They ruled out TB [tuberculosis] and sarcoidosis. Everything came back [saying that my shortness of breath was being caused by] silicosis."

There are three types of silicosis

- Acute silicosis - occurs due to short-term exposure to extremely elevated amounts of silica.
- Chronic silicosis - occurs due to exposure to large amounts of silica over a period of approximately five to ten years.
- Accelerated silicosis - occurs due to long-term exposure (10-20 years) to small amounts of silica.

Les was actually relieved with this diagnosis because, he figured, at least it wasn't cancer. He believed he could live with silicosis, going on to explain, "A person lives 10 to 15 years with silicosis, so that's not so bad. I figured at 10 to 15 years—or maybe longer on down the road, I'd really get bad [with shortness of breath]. It really didn't bother me.

"But see, mine [his particular type of silicosis] didn't take that long. Mine was at warp speed. Like Hawk's Nest."[4]

Leslie was slowly walking six miles a day in 1994, but the most important thing to him was that he could still go to work in the mine. By July of 1995, he could barely go two miles. A doctor told him that if he quit mining at that time, he might have another 2 more years to live—Les' expectation of living another 10 to 15 years was now gone. His worsening shortness of breath forced him into an early retirement in November of 1995. Two years later, in the fall of 1997, he was having trouble just walking from the bedroom to the living room. He was spending most of his days in bed, wearing oxygen all the time.

When asked what his life was like then, what was going through his mind, he answered, "Well, I was just taking it a day at a time. It bothered me because I couldn't play with my kids. I couldn't go hunting with my son. I couldn't go out with my daughter. I stayed at home."

And how about his relationship with Linda? In their region it is customary for men go out to earn a living while a wife stays home. "It was a big letdown. When I had to quit work everything just fell on her. She had to cut the grass, and go to work. And do everything around the house. It was hard to accept."

But even within the isolation and despair, Leslie would break another barrier by helping to create greater awareness of Black Lung Disease. In the spring of 1998 a major Kentucky newspaper published a series of highly acclaimed articles about Black Lung Disease. Les was featured in one of the stories, briefly touching upon his success in winning his battle with worker's compensation. The story also told about Leslie's painfully diminishing quality of life as he approached the final phase of a terminal disease.

157

Breaking Financial Barriers

To compound the stress of living with a critical respiratory problem, knowing that their only hope was a lung transplant, Les and Linda found out in 1995 that Les' government health insurance card was no longer accepted at office visits. Bills had to then be paid for through Linda's work insurance coverage.

Facing this, yet another indignity, Les was motivated to break down this barrier. He engaged in a four-month battle to receive payment from worker's compensation, enduring seemingly endless prods and pokes from doctors as well as an onslaught of prying questions from government lawyers. "Of course my family needed the money," Les said. "And these monthly compensation checks also let me feel like I was still able to contribute something to the support of my wife and children, the way a man ought to be able to do."

Only a very small (7.5 percent) of all applicants applying for federal Black Lung benefits are successful. Les was one of the lucky ones. As a result of his persistence he was awarded $779 monthly in worker's compensation from the federal government in April of 1996. This was a huge victory for Les, and more importantly, helped generate more awareness for the perilous plight of Black Lung victims.

Moreover, Les discovered that worker's compensation refused to provide payment for lung transplants (or anything related to transplant examination or evaluation), at that time still considered by workman's comp to be experimental. Les took it to court. In a landmark ruling, the judge ruled in Les' favor, saying that heart and lung transplants had become common enough to no longer be considered experimental. Breaking this enormous barrier, Leslie Blevins paved the way for improving the health of miners, being the first ever lung transplant in a coal miner to be covered by workmans' compensation.

December of 1999 came, and finally, with some good news. Les had been put on the list for a lung transplant! But the window of opportunity for lung transplants can sometimes be narrow, especially when the patient has a rapidly deteriorating condition as Les did. This is because the patient must be sick enough to require a new lung, but be strong enough to survive the transplant operation and to begin rehabilitation soon after.

Getting on the list was good news that gave Linda and Leslie hope. It also reinforced Linda's belief that God would provide. "I always felt at peace. I knew God was going to work some miracle. I didn't know what, but I never doubted Les would be OK." In a calm voice, in her slow drawl, Linda, rock steady, says, "There was never a doubt in my mind."

~~~~~~~~~~~~~~~~~~~~~

As part of a regular monthly routine, Linda and Les drove over 200 miles from Logan to Morgantown, to keep appointments with his pulmonary physician, Dr. Daniel Banks. Linda was now doing all the driving. For a proud man who was accustomed to being the breadwinner, providing for his family, and doing all the driving, this was yet another thing that was hard for Les to take.

After the four-hour drive, on April 7, 2000, their visit with doctor Banks was over in less than 30 minutes. And at the conclusion of the examination, the doctor's evaluation was most disheartening. "I hate to tell you, but you can't get the transplant because you don't qualify." Les' oximetry test had been so bad, he was now considered too sick, the silicosis too far advanced, for him to receive a new lung. Doctor Banks told Les, then only age 47, that he had about a week to live.

It might have looked like Les' death was imminent, but he was fated to break through more earthly barriers as part of his struggle to hold onto life. And of course through-out it all, Linda kept the faith and joined with her husband in this battle of a lifetime.

"We cried the whole way home," Les said. "I done give up. I was right with the Lord. I figured I was just gonna take everything in stride. There was nothing else I could do. I couldn't walk 10 feet without falling. I was using as much oxygen as I could take; 4 liters in my neck [transtracheal] and 6 in my nose. That was 10-12 altogether. You can't go any higher than that. If I got it, [the transplant] I got it. If I didn't, I didn't. I just wanted to see my grandkids."

Les had been especially close to one little grandson, Shawn. Although the little one was just a toddler, in Linda's words, "Shawn kept Les going. Even in times of great despair, he gave him the desire to go on. Les would be down and then we'd get a call that Shawn was coming over, and Les would perk right up. When they'd be playing and Les would get tired or get a coughing spell, Shawn would just quit. Then he'd wait until his 'papa' felt better. He saw the tube in Les' nose and seemed to know sometimes that 'papa' couldn't play. It was something. Then after Shawn had left, Les really looked forward to his next visit with us."

Back to the day when they learned Les could no longer be on the transplant list, Linda's reaction was, "All I could say was, the doctors may have given up—but God hasn't. In the Bible, God tells us, *'I will never leave you or forsake you.'* And every time something would happen, there would be a verse to follow that."

Les continues, "So we got home from the doctor. My grandkids were at the door 20 minutes later. We couldn't believe it. They had come all the way from Ohio. We hadn't called them. They just showed up."

But their time together was brief. Linda explained, "We had only been home two hours and a call came from the Cleveland Clinic. They were putting us on alert that a lung might be available. The people at the clinic were still going by Les' old test. So according to that one he was still eligible to receive the transplant."

Linda continues, "When you're on alert you get ready while they check if everything matches—you know, with your records and the new lung, the blood type and everything. If it is, you're ready to go. They did—and everything was a match. Our local ambulance company had been told a while back that if a call came from us to bring Les to the airport, he had to be their highest priority. So we called the ambulance service and then we had to wait two hours. There were so many wrecks that day. And there weren't even any ambulances on standby. Not a one. All the ambulances were out on calls."

"We learned later," Linda said, "That while we were waiting for an ambulance, the pilot was attending a church service. He was at a revival and his beeper went off. At first he thought he wouldn't answer it. It was such a good service. Then he decided he should answer his pager. But it [the delays] all worked out because as we were in the ambulance turning into the airport we saw the plane was just coming down the runway. The plane and the ambulance both arrived at the airport at the same time."

"We took off and we hit the storm. There was rain, sleet, snow, and hail." Les said, "It was 8pm. The temperature was 80 degrees at home. It was 30 degrees in Cleveland." Those differences in temperatures were causing a storm—a big raging Springtime storm. This was Linda's first time flying in an airplane.

Severe weather caused traffic controllers to direct the pilot to land in Akron, 45 minutes from the hospital. Linda feared that Les might not live through yet another leg of their journey. The pilot refused to go to Akron, deciding to fly 20 miles out and onto a different approach to Cleveland. Barely a minute from the runway the sky suddenly opened up and the clouds cleared. "It was just like God's hand came down and cleared away the clouds," says Les. "Then right after we landed, it just closed up again." A police officer, sent to the airport to escort them to the hospital, later told the Blevins that he had no idea how the plane managed to land in the violent storm. The officer said as he was driving to the airport, he could hardly see the road through the driving rain."

"How the Lord just moved on everything, it was amazing," Linda said as recalled that night. "Everything was just timed beautifully. It was a real miracle."

Les Blevins received a new left lung on April 8, 2000. The operation went very well. Dr. Malcolm DeCamp, the Louisville, Kentucky, native in charge of the clinic's lung transplant program, later told Les that when he removed his left lung, it was small enough to be held in the palms of his hands (a normal lung is the size of half your chest). The doctor said the lung was heavy, like concrete. It was that stiff and dense. A normal healthy lung is like fluffy sponge. Like angel food cake with a million tiny air sacs. Les' right lung, while in better condition but still affected by silicosis, was kept in place.

"I woke up about two days later. When I finally woke up, I said, 'Is it over?'" Les was asked what his very first thoughts were after the transplant operation. He laughs. "I was just glad to be there!"

Les doesn't know anything about the donor. He does know that a patient in the same room with him was also recovering from a transplant. He was the man who received the same donor's heart. The two men never really talked, but indeed, have a shared connection.

Linda says, "After the transplant, Les was in the hospital for 20 days. There was setback after setback after setback. He had to learn to walk again three times." But Linda's faith was never shaken. "I knew the Lord didn't bring him this far to take him away now." She says, "Even the public relations girl at the hospital in Cleveland—she said to me, 'It sounds like you *do* have a miracle!'"

Not long after the operation, Les' breathing capacity increased from 14 percent to 50 percent. Dr. DeCamp explained to Linda, "Since we only replaced one lung, I'm not expecting him to get to 100 percent. He should be well enough to breathe without bottled oxygen, walk without gasping for air, and spend time with his children and grand-children just like any other grandpa would. The most important thing is, he'll have a huge increase in the quality of his life. I'd love to see him to be able to go back to work." But as he later told Les, "I didn't put a new lung in you so you could go back to the mine."

It will be three years in April that Les received his new lung, his new life. "Over there [at Cleveland Clinic], they tell us, 'If you live the first six months, you can expect to live about 5 years.' We get newsletters, though, and some people have lived 9-10 years."

As of February 2003, Les is doing very well. He recently returned from a check-up in Cleveland and says, "Everything was looking good. My new lung is working at 90% capacity and my old lung is at 50%." Les takes 28 pills a day. "I was on 48. This is medicine I'll be on for the rest of my life." He was asked about experiencing side effects from all this medicine. "I have trembles. That's it. So far that's all."

Les was asked what he would like people to learn, to know, from his experience. His answer was three-fold.

"A lot of people are not organ donors because they're afraid that when the doctor sees their driver's license, he won't work on them, thinking that just one body could help save so many lives. They think he says, 'I'll lose this one, but I'll save maybe 20 other people.' That's not true. The doctors want you to know that they'll work hard to give everybody *every* chance."

"Also, a lot of people think, 'I don't have money. They give organs to a rich person.'"

"And that's not true."

"No, it's not."

Finally, Les wants the miners to know and understand this: "The coal miners, they used to think that nothing could be done [to help them]. A lot of them just won't pursue it. But we fought for it [compensation], and we've set a precedent. I want them to know this. And I'll do anything I can to help."

Breaking barriers, keeping the faith, helping others, and having so many of the experiences that Leslie and Linda have had is amazing. But in September, 2000, with the help of a new lung, Leslie Blevins did something very common, yet truly wonderful. Another miracle took place as he, a proud father, participated in a special family event. Les walked his daughter, Lynn, down the aisle to meet her groom. It is well known that loved ones may tend to shed a tear or two as a bride enters the church and marches down the aisle. But Linda says, on that day, "There was not a dry eye in the church. It was a beautiful wedding, and everybody knew what it meant."

Leslie, Shawn, and Linda
before transplant

Les and his daughter, Lynn, on her wedding day.

One year transplant anniversary celebration.
Les, Linda, son Bryan, and daughter Lynn
on the top of a mountain in the Smokies.

Life in Coal Country

Joan Savilla and Sammie Wade were young girls growing up in coal country. Although they were not miners, their stories give you some idea of what it is like to grow up in the midst of this hazardous environment. As this book went to print, Sammie reported that she has fibrosis in both lungs, possibly caused by an auto-immune disease. As a child she was exposed to a lot of second hand smoke as well.

Many thanks to Betty Dotson-Lewis for sharing these accounts. Joan and Sammie's stories can be found in their entirety at www.Appalachianpower.com.
(Click on "oral histories.")

Coal Camp Memories
by Joan Savilla

I was born in a small coal-mining town called Highcoal, West Virginia. Mom said that the coal tipple [the place where coal-loaded cars are emptied by tipping] was situated practically over the top of our little four-room house. On a couple of occasions I have gone back to try to find some evidence of my birth-place. However, time and the elements have removed it from the face of the earth.

When we were growing up, we moved from place to place, following Daddy's work. First, up one "holler" and then the next. We lived in lots of these little coal towns and shopped at the infamous "coal company store." I remember one little house we lived in was about ten feet from the railroad track. It was in a little town called "Keith" in Boone County. I think all the little houses had four rooms, a porch and an outhouse. Sometimes in the dead of winter, the inside of the house could almost be as cold as the outhouse.

I had a real penchant for bananas as a child. Of course, we never had enough money to buy them, and the only time I got one was at someone else's house or at school. Once when I was out playing near the company store, I noticed that the banana crates were placed behind the store after the "Surface Banana" truck ran. I investigated the crates, secretly hoping that they had forgotten a banana or two in the crate. They were packed in a lightweight type of straw or packing material. I carefully slid my hands through all the straw in each of the banana boxes. Oh, it was my lucky day! I found two or three bananas. After that, I anxiously awaited the Surface Banana truck every week. I would wait around until I was sure that no one was watching, and then I would go on my treasure hunt looking for bananas. I don't recall how long I continued this practice, but am still reminded of it many times when I eat bananas.

When Daddy came home from work, he was covered with coal dust from head to foot. Mom always had hot water ready on our big coal cook stove. We had a round galvanized tub that was used for bathing. Daddy was a fairly large man, and I think he pretty much filled that tub up before the water was poured in. Mom would help him bathe, washing his back and the places he couldn't get to. When he emerged from the bedroom where the bath had taken place, he still had those tell-tale raccoon eyes that marked him as a coal miner. We girls would help him finish the job of cleaning his face. We would meticulously go over his face and neck to make sure that he was clean, keeping the coal dust out of the pores of his skin.

The summertime in a coal camp was loads of fun for us kids. We played from sun-up to sunset and never ran out of things to do. It was rare to find an overweight kid in camp. We either didn't get enough to eat, or we played so hard that we ran it off before it could become fat. We had no shoes in the summer. It was hard enough for Mom and Dad to put shoes on our feet in the fall to start school. I would like to have a nickel for every time I stumped my toe, stepped on a rock, or cut my feet during the summertime. Although our feet toughened up considerably, they were still vulnerable to such things.

When dusk fell in the coal camp, neighbors could be seen out in their yards or on the porch enjoying the summer evenings. The children were out in the street, playing ball, having foot races, or the girls would be playing house on someone's porch with their dolls and little brothers and sisters. We didn't use insect spray in those days. Everyone had their own insect repellent in their yard. It was called a "gnat smoke." It was an old can in which a rag soaked with some kind of solvent was lit with a match. It didn't flame up and burn out quickly—it smoked for hours. The smoke from this little invention kept the bugs away. Up and down the narrow street, smoke from the little cans permeated the hot, sultry, summer air in the coal camp.

Life was tough on Mom and Dad during those days, but we children didn't know it. They always seemed to find time to laugh with us and spend time with us. Dad was always puttering around on the little house fixing this or that. Mom was always going to a bare cupboard and miraculously managing to put something on the table for us to eat. We ate beans and cornbread or biscuits most every day. We never asked for something different when we went to the table, or refused to eat because we didn't like it. We ate it and were glad to get it. It was rare that we had anything to drink other than water. Sometimes we had Kool-Aid, but most of the time we drank water. We started drinking coffee at an early age, because Daddy loved it and thought nothing of giving us a cup of coffee when we were children. He also thought nothing of teaching us to smoke cigarettes. He had a cigarette roller with the little white cigarette papers and Prince Albert tobacco in a can. When he wanted a smoke, we would fight over who was going to roll it for him and light it. All seven of us children smoked cigarettes at one time or another.

Daddy died in October, 1993. He had black lung and emphysema. The last fifteen years of his life was spent sitting in his rocking chair. He spent the day just trying to get one good breath of air. His heart finally could manage no longer and he died quietly in his sleep at 78 years of age. Mom died in July 2001, also at the age of 78. Two "beacons of light" from the great generation of hard working people passed from this life, leaving seven children who became hard workers and caring people; people who lived through the tough times of being the children of a West Virginia coal miner and his wife, carrying with them the memories of life in the coal camps.

Memories of Welch

by Sammie Wade

My mother, Ethel Wade was born in Davy, West Virginia in 1912. She was the daughter of a Baldwin-Felts agent who worked as an enforcer for the mine owners. When my father, an officer with the 65th Infantry Division was shipped to Europe soon after my birth, my mother and I returned to McDowell County to stay with my aunt and uncle. My brief time with them was a magical time for me. Even now, when I am awakened by the rattle of the Amtrak train that runs near my Florida home, I recall the train whistles echoing through the hollows near Welch, the smell of my uncle's cigar, and my aunt's Blue Grass cologne. My uncle was a pharmacist and the owner of the Citizen's Drugstore.

When my mother and I came to live in McDowell County, the world was at war, and McDowell County was an important part of the war effort because it mined the coal that literally fueled the war effort. Almost everyone had a loved one whose life was in peril because of the war. Many consumer goods were strictly rationed. Much of the world was on the brink of the Apocalypse. But no more than a toddler, I was oblivious to this. The only grief I knew was the daily one that occurred when my dear aunt and uncle left for work.

Every day I spent many hours at the back window of the apartment watching the trains go by. In those days, the tracks ran right along the river and through the center of town. The railroad engineers were heroes to me. Just as children now may idolize fighter pilots or astronauts, I worshiped railroad engineers. I waved at them as I sat at the window, and many of them waved back at me. One day after I had a bath and was dressed in my finest, Mother and I started to walk downtown to the drugstore. As we neared the tracks, I spied a stopped train and recognized the engineer as one who regularly returned my wave. He must have recognized me too, because he motioned us over and lifted me into the cab of the train engine. He let me spend a few blissful minutes pretending that I was the engineer before handing me, encrusted with coal dust, back to my horrified mother.

On Saturday mornings my uncle would put me in the car and take me to Brown's Creek to feed sugar cubes to the mules that worked in the mines. But my happiest moments were spent in the Citizen's Drug. They would hoist me up to the soda fountain and let me mix my own fountain Coca-Colas with enough Coca-Cola syrup in each for a whole six pack of today's Coke.

At age three, fun and games were over me. My uncle put me to work. We sold cigarettes, which someone had to unpack and stack in bins very close to the floor. Since I was cheap labor and short, that became my job. The only problem was that it required a modicum of reading ability to sort the cigarettes by brand. So, at age three I began learning to read with a vocabulary consisting solely of words like Camel, Lucky Strike, and Old Gold.

Finally, my father, James Wade returned safely from Europe. He was a stranger to me, and the last thing I wanted to do was to leave with him. My mother and I went back to Virginia with him, and I never returned to Welch to live. Every summer I would board the Powhatan Arrow and wind my way back to Welch to the place that would always be my home, where I was always welcomed and loved.

In the 1960's I spent the summer at Grace Hospital watching my uncle die of cancer. In 1985 I returned to get my aunt to take her home with me where she died of lung cancer. I flew her body back to Welch for her funeral at the Presbyterian Church. I packed her belongings and began the long drive, alone, back to Florida. As I drove out of Welch, I saw a sign that said "Davy, 5 miles." I pulled to the side of the road and hesitated. I figured I might never return and maybe should visit the place it all began, to the place my mother was born. In the end the pain was too great, and I just drove on.

Section Six

Things That Make it Worse

"Pray that God will help you accept your condition."
Edwin Brubaker, Sterling Heights, MI

The Big "D"

*"Don't sit around and do nothing.
The more you do, the more you will do.
And listen to your doctor."*

Betty Roemer, Detroit, MI

Denial. It has been defined as disbelief in the existence or reality of a thing and refusal to recognize or acknowledge, a disowning or disavowal of an existing condition.

In my work, and moreover in researching this book, I found that denial is very common in people with chronic pulmonary disease. In stories told to me, the denial theme kept appearing, woven through much of what each person said about their struggle with shortness of breath. In fact, I discovered that with most people a period of denial, silent and / or expressed, is a part of the sometimes lengthy process of acceptance.

Thus far you've met several people in this book. Here is what some of them had to say.

Sheila Shiel said, **"Yes, denial is fun...I kept waiting for my 'bronchitis' to go away, swallowing antibiotic** after antibiotic. [The concept of having] emphysema never penetrated...however, I knew all about asthma. When they said I had COPD, I said, 'What is that?' But really I was forever in denial despite a collapsed lung, bronchoscope procedures, multiple pneumonias, and finally...disability. Now I know, but never really understood before, that the combination of various lung diseases is what makes it COPD, and is what causes the extent of damage, deterioration, and illness."

Denial can be very powerful. It can lead to problems that go further than just the denial itself and impact the lives of people other than the person living with the disease.

Mary Pierce said, "The denial was definitely there, and I was part of the isolation for a *long* time. It was like I was the only one that had *the secret*. It's like I was carrying a huge dark secret. At least I felt that way, and I was hiding it from everybody. That alone prevented some of the close personal interactions... the wall was up, even with my family. I was denying it and hiding it, and that was part of who I was. So I was hiding it from my family. The interactions became artificial. You know, pretending."

During that time Mary became very clever in developing techniques prompted by her denial. She was always able to come up with a plausible reason not to do something.

"I remember back when I could not do much of anything. I just didn't have the energy to do it. I'd say, 'I can't. I've got to go do this or I've got to do that.' I'd just make an excuse somehow."

When asked if she thought her husband, Todd, knew that something was wrong, Mary answered, "He says he didn't. When people later asked him, 'Didn't you know that something was going on?' He answered, 'Well, I knew she was losing a lot of weight, but it just happened so gradually, I never noticed [the increasing shortness of breath].' Because, again, he was making all the little incremental adjustments along the way."

Denial can also adversely affect a patient's relationship with his or her physician. There can be no partnership in effective medical treatment and lung health management if the doctor is unaware of breathing problems in the patient.

Consequently, without the correct and proper information, it is not possible to make informed end-of-life decisions regarding life support, or "heroic" measures. More than anybody, the person with chronic disease needs to discuss end-of-life issues with their family in order that they may make informed decisions together. The decisions must then be written down and placed where medical personnel and family can find them. Not doing so puts a great burden on family members who are faced not only with making difficult decisions at a time of crisis, but need to make those decisions in light of a chronic diagnosis that to them—because of the mask of denial—now seems so new.

So why deny? The patient's energy level is already *so low*! Why work *so hard* at denying this disease? Why add to the stress by fighting acceptance?

In her book *The Chronic Illness Experience,* Cheri Register says, "It is not so much fear and denial as it is confusion and embarrassment that keep people out of the doctor's office in the early stages of illness. Having no clear sense of the boundaries that divide illness from health, we redraw our own as needed to keep ourselves functioning."

Mary Pierce said, "The hiding. The secret. The shame. *Guilt.* Does it make sense?"

Did Mary feel this way because she believed she did it to herself by years of smoking cigarettes?

"You know, I'd see other people with health problems, worse than mine, things they didn't bring on themselves. I figured I'd shortened my life and all that. *I did it to myself.* At the time I didn't think it all the way through, but my reaction then was guilt, shame, embarrassment.

Shame can keep a person from accepting their diagnosis. It is very hard to admit that a horrible disease may have been brought on by something done voluntarily.

Whatever we call it, fear, denial, confusion, embarrassment, though chronic lung disease symptoms may temporarily subside, they eventually demand attention.

With denial there is no diagnosis. With no diagnosis there is no treatment, and with no treatment chronic lung disease, and one's overall health, will only get worse. Denial of the existence of CLD can lead to a person having both more treatment and less treatment than needed. Treating each exacerbation as an isolated case, as just another "bout of bronchitis," can mean over prescribing of antibiotics. Failure to treat CLD symptoms at all, on the other hand, denies the patient the opportunity to benefit from helpful medications, education, support, and exercise that can extend and improve the quality of life.

Mary says, "There are millions of people with chronic lung disease who are not listening to their bodies, not hearing what the doctor has to say, or not finding a doctor who is knowledgeable enough or who cares enough to say what needs to be said."

In some cases the diagnosis has been given, but understated by the doctor. Some patients are told by their doctor that they have a "little touch" of emphysema. This might even be considered denial on the part of the physician!

"Those words 'a little touch' kind of put the patient on notice that they don't have to worry about it. Hearing a wishy-washy diagnosis and prognosis is like going into confessional and being forgiven."

It is also important to be able to understand that in all but a few cases, the disease has been progressing for quite some time, probably for years or even decades. A classic scenario, especially involving those affected with emphysema, is that the patient states that they were just fine until recently coming down with pneumonia. Upon further examination (chest x-ray, pulmonary function, arterial blood gas, and personal health history) it becomes abundantly clear to the doctor and, eventually to the patient, that lung disease has been present for many years. As the lungs become more and more compromised over time they are less able to tolerate common insults such as colds and flu. To the person who feels they were fine until a recent illness and is now told they have 30% lung function left (70% non-functional and beyond repair), it is like being hit with the proverbial ton of bricks.

Cheri Register sheds some light on this, saying, "We continue to tell these stories [of when the illness began] because it seems important to have a frame in which to contain the experience of chronic illness. The story needs a strong beginning because it has no structure otherwise. With chronic illness, there is no single climax, just the irregularly recurring ups and downs...Chronic illness does not fit the popular notion of how illness proceeds: 'You get sick, you go to the doctor and get some medicine, and wait to get better'... The best we can do to clear up the chaos in our lives is to look back and say, 'This is how it all began. This was when my life took an unfortunate turn.'"

Finally, and so importantly, just because a person admits and accepts the diagnosis of chronic lung disease it does not mean that he or she is about to give up. Far from it! Acceptance gives a person the permission and the *power* to acquire knowledge—knowledge that will arm them with weapons needed for the battle to fight their disease. With the help of a good physician and referrals to a pulmonary specialist and a pulmonary rehabilitation program, the person with chronic lung disease can begin the process of learning so much about breathing better and living well.

New life begins again on the day of acceptance for the person with chronic lung disease. With the help and support from understanding health care professionals as well as knowledgeable peers, the patient can learn what works and what doesn't, what is achievable and what isn't, what is realistic and what is no longer safe to attempt. Once free from the grip of denial, the patient can gain control of breathing, again with hope for the best possible life from that moment on.

When Should You Seek Help?

Cheri Register says, "The first challenge any illness poses is in deciding just when you are sick enough to worry about it. Often the initial problems are not that great a departure from your usual state of health. As annoying as they might be, you may be tempted to dismiss them, unless they are known to be danger signals, like the [more well-known] 'warning signs of cancer.' Everyone has aches and pains, after all, and most of them subside on their own. For fear of being called hypochondriacs, many of us would rather wait out the discomfort than risk seeming excessively alarmed."

Could You Have COPD?

- Are you 45 or older, currently smoke cigarettes or have smoked in the past?

- Are you 45 or older and have a history of breathing irritants in your environment?

- Do you sometimes have coughing fits or breathing trouble when exerting?

- Do you have frequent bouts of bronchitis?

- Do you cough up mucus or phlegm in the morning?

- Does asthma, bronchitis, or emphysema run in your family?

If you answered "yes" to any of these questions, you might have COPD. Ask your doctor about taking a simple spirometry (lung function) test. This test takes only a few minutes. Visit www.nlhep.org (The National Lung Health Education Program) for more information.

My Faithful Friends, My Cigarettes

"Learn how to live all over again and it is worth it."
Betty Biondi, Detroit, MI

Not everybody with Chronic Lung Disease has smoked cigarettes, but most have. And many of them smoked a lot. Let's face it: smoking damages the lungs.

Why do people smoke? Why do they continue to smoke long after it becomes apparent that smoking is so bad for their health? There are many reasons. Here are some of the most common ones. *By no means is cigarette smoking condoned here. I simply believe that it is important to face the attraction of cigarettes in order to understand the grip they have on the smoker.*

It is also important to mention that while friends and relatives may be sympathetic and empathetic toward loved ones who are afflicted with arthritis, diabetes, or other chronic illnesses, they often tend to feel that the person with emphysema has "done this to himself or herself." Thus chronic lung disease patients are challenged not only by the disease itself, but also by sometimes critical, unsympathetic attitudes of others.

183

➤ Why Do People Smoke? ➤

Cigarettes are a comfort. Smoking cigarettes can somehow seem to help a person both relax *and* feel more energetic. A woman once told me that her cigarettes were her friends. She could always count on them to be there when she felt down and lonely. When she quit smoking she grieved their loss. She felt alone, as if she had lost close friends.

Cigarettes go with coffee. Many people feel that for them, the smoke goes right along with the coffee and having one without the other is impossible. Some people, albeit some more than others, seem to need that "kick" in the morning. They feel they need to use something to get themselves going. When people stop smoking they often, at least for a while, have to stop drinking coffee. One does not taste good any more without the other. There was once a lady in our pulmonary rehab program who had suffered tremendous hardship, at age four losing her entire family and her village to war. By the time she was in her 50's she had lived all over the world. She spoke four languages. She told me that she could be at a table with complete strangers anywhere in the world and if they were all drinking coffee and smoking cigarettes, there was an unspoken kinship that made her feel comfortable and at home.

Smoking cigarettes was in the past looked upon by many as simply "the thing to do." Before the Surgeon General's warning began reaching the general public in the 1960's, most people never thought of cigarette smoking as dangerous. It was a very common and acceptable thing to do. Almost all of my father's friends smoked. My grandfather began smoking at age 11. When I met my husband he smoked three packs a day. Smoking was something, simply, that teenage boys and men just did. I once had a patient who told me that his father took him behind the shed at age 12 and said, "It's time you start smoking. You're a man."

Smoking is considered by some young people to be "cool." An estimated 3000 teenagers begin smoking each day. Ninety percent of adults who smoke started by age 21 and had become regular smokers by their eighteenth birthday. [5]

⤳ Continuing to Smoke:
Walking Tightrope without a Net ⤳

So why do people continue to smoke? Why do they keep on doing something that causes such ill health? Why do they put their money and their breath into a little white stick that at one time may have helped them feel glamorous or been their companion in times of terrific stress; but has now betrayed them so dreadfully? There's no doubt about it. Cigarettes have a grip on the person who smokes. Remember, nobody gets out of bed at three in the morning, in the winter, wearing bedroom slippers and their coat over pajamas, to drive to the convenience store to buy cigarettes simply because they love to smoke. That person is hooked. Nicotine meets the criteria of an addictive drug. [6]

Continuing to smoke after one knows that it is detrimental to their health might even *seem*, to that person, to temporarily help with anger and depression; ironically the depression that quite often comes with chronic lung disease. At any rate continuing to smoke does *not* help, but leads to even further problems.

For the person continuing to smoke, appointments with the pulmonary doctor might be canceled, or the patient might be less than honest with their physician concerning their smoking status. If the appointment is kept the patient knows exactly what he or she is going to hear the doctor say, "You have to quit smoking." This is a difficult thing to hear when the patient feels like he or she absolutely cannot quit.

When discussing her inability to quit smoking. Mary Pierce says, "That's probably why I didn't go to the doctor."

Social withdrawal may begin. Friends might make negative comments about the person still smoking. "Is Joe still smoking? Just listen to that cough! I quit cold turkey. If a person *really* wants to quit, they can just put their cigarettes down and never pick them up again." This type of reaction is understandable, but if the patient who smokes feels there is no support in becoming a successful quitter, he or she might experience feelings of depression and failure. "Why quit? The damage is done. Everybody is on my case. Smoking is the only thing I have left." Continuing to smoke is not only dangerous, but can erode what little physical and emotional support remains.

Furthermore, if the patient *is* successful in quitting, sometimes he or she may actually feel worse, healthwise, for a while after ceasing to smoke. He or she may get a cold, cough more and produce more phlegm, or gain weight. That person then might think, "Why bother? I'm doing worse *now* than when I was smoking."

➤ Getting Support ➤

So what is the smoker to do? It is absolutely essential to have empathetic support along with education and understanding. **Support and understanding of the smoker / quitter can make the difference in staying quit.** The person must know that quitting is quite possibly the hardest thing they will ever have to do. But it can be done! And it *must* be done even though it seems at times as if the quitter will climb the walls!

There are several options available to the person who is ready to quit. Start with asking a physician about them. But don't stop there. Support, education, and understanding are available in a variety of quit smoking programs. Help can also be found in Better Breathers' Clubs, Pulmonary Rehabilitation, and mentoring, as well as on line. Advice and understanding mean the most when they come from someone who has fought the same battle.

This is a note of encouragement from Linda to a woman who contacted a COPD internet support group regarding her smoking mother:

"Dear 'Joan',
I can certainly relate with your mother as far as fear [of quitting] goes. I was afraid to give up cigarettes as they were my best friends, I thought, and an hour without one seemed impossible. I learned to do without one for five minutes at a time early on. You have a desire to smoke, but it goes away whether you smoke or not. That's how I got through it. I agree with [Betty] who said if it were easy, everyone would quit. It was the hardest thing I ever did, but that keeps some of the guilt in check... I think she [your mother] is so lucky to have a caring and considerate daughter like you. Remember that she will go though many emotions and she should feel free to express them. Don't let her keep her fears to herself... Good luck to both of you."
Linda in Pittsburgh

Here is an on line letter of support from Arlene to Kay:

"Hi Kay! Just wanted to let you know that the craving does lessen. The more time that goes by, the less the urge. For me, it was hard to get past that hand-mouth thing. So, I stuffed my mouth with hard candy and food, not the best way...just substituting one addiction for another.

"When I quit, Labor Day, 1984, I didn't know that the car would start without a cigarette, or that I could talk on the phone without one. Tea, alone? ... without a butt? Impossible! But that passed. For a long time after I quit, I had the smoking dream... the one where I would light up and wake up in a panic, breaking out into a cold sweat. It was before my COPD diagnosis... during my long denial period, and yet... even then, I knew that one more butt would kill me because there was no such thing as only 'one.'

"Today, I very rarely get the urge except after I put the Thanksgiving turkey in the oven... [in years past] that was the time I would sit for a few minutes, feet up, and light up....a short break before beginning the rest of the cooking. For the last three years, we've gone to a dear friend for that holiday...no more urges for that day!

"Seriously, it really does pass...it's just hard to see when recovery is so new...Just take it one day at a time... it's the only way to survive it!

Health!"

Arlene

Mary Pierce felt a great sense of relief when she was told that her lung disease was inherited and not caused completely by smoking. "Oh, God, I *didn't* do this entirely to myself. Now I felt like I could face people. But I was still smoking these stupid cigarettes. Knowing that this was happening and still not being able to quit smoking. I mean, it was stupid. It was absolutely stupid."

And Mary also struggled with that feeling of futility. The "why bother?"

"You dummy, you did this to yourself and the damage is done. Oh, what the hell have another cigarette."

John Widmayer quit smoking three times before his success would last. "The first time, I threw my cigarettes out the car window. I just threw them out. And I went through all the cravings for about six months. The second time I took a Smoke Stoppers class through work. The third time, I went out and bought a pound of candy. You know, all the mixed candies you buy in bulk. Every time I craved a cigarette, I'd have a piece of candy. I never really liked sweets. About half way through the second pound, I just quit. That was it. I quit for good."

Finally, here is a letter to all the new quitters in a COPD on-line support group. The cheerleader is Janie in Sacramento, CA.

"Hello Everyone,

"It has been a week now since you had that last cigarette. And this isn't the letter that I had prepared for the first anniversary week for new non-smokers. The original was pretty typical jargon, you know, the 'atta girl and 'atta boy routine.

"Then yesterday I heard the results of a Pulmonary Function test from one of my best friends who recently celebrated her 60th birthday. Due primarily to not being able to stop smoking, her [lung] volume had dropped 10% in the past 2 1/2 years. She had felt so guilty about smoking that she canceled checkups with her pulmonary doctor until she stopped three months ago.

"It made me wonder how highly intelligent men and women could fall prey to a tobacco leaf that only an insect would eat. It made me wonder how easy it is for us to say, 'I'll think about that tomorrow' or 'I'll stop as a New Year's resolution *next* year.' It made me wonder why we ignored the warning signs. It made me wonder about a lot of things we would rather not confront.

"For all of you out there who are 'hanging in there,' you should be very proud of what you are doing for yourselves and for your families. If you temporarily fail, dust yourself off and get back up again. *But don't stop trying!*

"Playing solitaire in your bathrobe 24 / 7 is better than O_2 24 / 7. Eating carrot sticks, lemon drops, jelly beans, or carrying a glass of water everywhere is better than having a cigarette. I once knew a CEO who ate toothpicks after he gave up smoking. He nibbled them and then spit out the little pieces of wood during board meetings. Disgusting to eat wood? And okay to ingest tobacco smoke? Well, you decide.

"Just don't give up! We are cheering for all of you... those of you who were brave enough to come out and admit to everyone that you were trying to quit, and those of you who are quietly trying to stop in your own way. We are here to help you to find a better life than tobacco can give you. Remember, it is fine to drop us a private note if you feel the need for instant support. We're listening!"

Quitting smoking might be the hardest thing you'll ever do, but it will also be one of the best, if not *the* best thing you'll ever do for yourself. Many people *have* been able to successfully break nicotine's grip. Begin by talking to your doctor and checking with local stop smoking resources. Then seek support from others who have quit. It can be done. *You can do it! Call* **1-800-LUNG-USA (1-800-586-4872)**

Janie (in Sacramento, CA) Gillette

Relationships

Voices of the Caregiver / Well Spouse

"Love each other as unconditionally as humanly possible."
Mary Van Langevelde

As with many aspects of our lives so closely tied to emotional well being, relationships we have and the interactions with those people closest to us can sometimes be of help—and can sometimes make things worse. Here are the stories of three families that will provide some insight for you and your loved one on your journey of living with chronic lung disease. This is not so much a discussion about who takes out the garbage, but how these families have coped, each in their own way, with the profound changes in daily routines, as well as in feelings, brought on by CLD.

The term 'well spouse' may be new to you. The difference between a caregiver and a well spouse is that a caregiver is *any* person who provides direct care to a person. He or she may be spouse, a family member, or a friend. The well spouse is the *spouse* of the person with the illness.

A caregiver or well spouse might say:

"Where do I draw the line? What should I do for my spouse and what should I let her do on her own?"

"Really, how bad is the shortness of breath? Sometimes I wonder if it is just an excuse for getting out of work."

"I just wish he would get up and move around. Then he might feel better. He just sits there!"

"I get so tired. You know, I'm not so young myself. Sometimes I feel like I am doing everything."

"I told him to quit smoking, but he didn't. And look at him. He ruined his lungs and now I've got to do everything for him."

A person with a chronic illness might say:

"Unless a person is in this situation they have *no* idea what it's like to be so short of breath."

"Sure, I feel sorry for my spouse having to do so much to take care of me, but she's got to understand that if I only could, I would love to do more for myself."

"I know the smoking did it. Don't people understand that I feel bad enough that I brought this on myself?"

"I'm still a person, you know. Sometimes people just treat me like an invalid."

Sound familiar? These questions and feelings are often voiced by people with CLD and by those closest to them. For many people, especially men who came of age in the 1940's and 1950's, self-worth is often measured by what they "do", more so than by who they are or what they feel. For many years they have been hard workers and providers, caring for and doing things for those whom they love and hold responsibility. When their ability to physically do things is lessened, they may feel, so is their self worth lessening.

The relationship with those people closest to them has also been changed by the illness.

How can the caregiver / well spouse possibly understand what it is like to have trouble breathing and to live in fear of it getting worse when they themselves have never had Chronic Lung Disease? And how can people cope with the changes in relationships brought on by a debilitating disease? Every situation is different, of course, but there are things we can all learn from looking at the ways in which chronic illness has affected these relationships.

Patrick's Story

"My lady passed away from a CO_2 [high carbon dioxide level] induced coma. She was only 47 and had very severe emphysema. When she died she was only 80 pounds, just skin and bones. I initially met her through my local Better Breathers' Club. One day she looked so sad. She said that her husband of 17 years had walked out and had asked for a divorce. She was absolutely devastated.

"I befriended her and we became very close friends. I was appalled at her home environment. She had two adult children; one was still living at home. The other was married and lived across town. She was trying to take care of her invalid father who was living in her home. My friend's son who lived at home was in total denial of his mother's condition. He did what he wanted and came and went as he wanted. He had no job and did not hesitate in asking Mom for money when he needed it. Her daughter was living across town with her husband. She had severed her ties with her mom because she and her husband got tired of the calls to help with this or that.

"Bottom line, *failure to face the realities of emphysema had torn that family apart.* Denial was rampant and my friend was working with little or no help just to survive. I tried to do what I could by just getting her away from the house. A little motorcycle drive in the country would help to brighten her spirits.

"When she passed away, some very dear friends from our Better Breathers Club started a local chapter of the Well Spouse Foundation in our community in my lady's memory. We were amazed when we found how many folks were trying to cope with someone in their own family who had a chronic illness. From people trying to cope with lung disease, to cancer, to multiple sclerosis and lots of others, we saw that there were many aging parents, spouses, or children who needed to be cared for. A caregiver has the unenviable task of trying to meet the sick one's needs and still take care of his or herself. "When one is sick, two need help!!

"In working with this group it gave to me great satisfaction to be in a position to help others, to suggest places and organizations that might help, and to offer a place to vent so they could talk about their trials and tribulations. One help is respite care. This is temporary care while the main caregiver can get out to attend a well spouse meeting or just go see a movie or get their hair done. Taking an occasional break from being a caregiver 24 hours a day helps to relieve the stress and strain. As organizers of the group we were able to help quite a few individuals get through a difficult time. Upon occasion, the sick one would pass away. Then that caregiver could move on, knowing that they gave it their best."

Dave's Story

Although not typical of classic COPD cases in which the patient is a person in their 50's, 60's, or 70's much can be learned from our friends and their well spouses affected by Alpha-1 Antitrypsin Deficiency (A-1AT is inherited emphysema). Alpha patients face mortality at an early age, and usually by the time the disease is diagnosed, it is very severe. Finding treatment becomes an urgent matter. Treatment must often happen in the midst of a life filled with career, young children, and home.

Dave's wife, Shirley, was 29 years old and Dave was 32. They were the parents of five young children, the oldest, age 10, the youngest, one year-old twins. Shirley was a nurse, Dave a businessman. Finding it harder and harder to breathe, and unable to lift or bathe the twins, Shirley knew she was in trouble. She weighed 88 pounds. Her lung function tests revealed a loss of 70% of normal function. She was diagnosed with Alpha-1 and thought her life was over. Following are excerpts from an interview with Dave.

What was your reaction to the diagnosis?

"Concern for her, our kids, our *life*. The diagnosis happened in stages. The first was emphysema. Not all that unexpected for a smoker, which Shirley was. My concern was less [at that time] since she could quit smoking and at least stop the damage from worsening. Her doctor then screened her for A-1AT because of the amount of damage her lungs had sustained. When the diagnosis came back, I was totally unprepared. I was hoping that it was all some medical mistake, and that everything would somehow be OK..."

Were you angry?

"I was at first, extremely angry."

At whom, or what?

"I just hated life in general. Felt betrayed by God. After a while I realized I was feeling normal emotions. Eventually I developed some relationships with a few key individuals with whom I could really vent my true emotions without feeling judged. I also went to rejoin the Catholic Church... It's (anger) easier to understand when you finally reach that point of acceptance of a genetic defect that happened by chance, than looking for blame.

"I felt *cheated* out of growing old with my wife, *angry* that my kids would have to experience death at such a young age. Just cheated by life in general.

"I first heard the diagnosis when I got a phone call while at work. I rushed out of the building and broke into tears. My friend Bob came out and listened to me sob like a baby. The worst part was having to face all the questions from people as I went back inside."

Were you embarrassed about crying or did you just not want to talk about it?

"No, I don't think it was a feeling of embarrassment. The reality was that I had no answers to give [my co-workers] except that I was told my wife would die. Not really a topic I wanted to discuss.

"I had questions that I needed to figure out for myself, and although my friends meant well, I heard the pity in their voices and I wanted to just lash out. I distinctly remember snapping at a very dear friend, Chris. She approached me the next day and told me how sorry she was to hear about my wife. As she spoke her eyes welted. I snapped at her and told her that I couldn't handle her crying and walked away. That is not my nature, and looking back it was a very insensitive thing to do. But I remember those lessons as I meet new well spouses and see the anger or disappointment in their eyes."

So, in that case, one of a new diagnosis, what is the best thing to say?

"It's not what you *say*, but more important, to listen. Let them know of the availability of an open ear, that help is there. The emotions are still so new and don't make sense. Fear of the unknown is so great and answers are so few. Stay away from 'I know exactly how you feel,' unless you really do. Don't try to force them to tell you things if they're not ready.

"When people tried to cheer me up, it just frustrated me because I wanted to tell them that this disease sucked, I hated it, and I was having a hard time coping. That didn't match their 'You're so strong, and you're dealing with this so well, better than I would' statements. In fact, I was struggling to cope with it all.

Now, having been in that situation, what do you say to the well spouses?

"I recently called a person who two weeks before I knew only on a casual basis. I had heard that her husband was diagnosed with cancer. I had heard [at the office] that she was a real trooper and handling it all so very well. When I called her and asked how *she* was doing, she spent twenty minutes telling me how her husband was (we all seem to develop a standard press release because we are asked so often).

"Eventually we talked about her worst fear, which was that her husband may die. She was worried about the future. She was tired, angry, and trying to do everything herself because that is what loving spouses do. She was barely eating because she didn't have the time. Her days were long and all her focus was on her husband. When she went to bed, she couldn't sleep because her mind wouldn't shut down. Many of her friends had already stopped coming over, and if they did they were there to see her husband. She had two children, boys, ages 15 and 8 who were afraid that dad was going to die and thought that cancer was contagious. She was caught in the middle with no manual to guide her. I told her that what she was feeling was normal. This seemed to help more than anything."

Did you ever ask, "Why me? Why us?"

"Quite frankly, the answer is no. I know that the typical answer is to ask those questions early on. I did play the 'Why her?' game... I did think, 'What about the kids? How will they react, and how will I respond? How can I raise them alone?'

"Death seemed to be a very real reality at that point, and one that I seemed to dwell on... This seems to be an important step in the grieving process. You grieve for the loss of your normal life, the loss of your spouse's health, and the loss of your children's normal childhood."

Dave and I discussed some of the emotions that have played a part in his life with Shirley and Alpha-1.

"Angry with Shirl? Yes. I wanted to be there for her and she shut me out. In the past I could tell her anything and now faced with the worst thing in my life, the one person who I could talk to about any problem, was the problem.

"Depressed about Shirley? Yes. Proud of her? Yes. Helpless? Yes. The feeling of helplessness is one of frustration, feeling like nothing matters anymore. [Their financial burden was enormous.] About the only interest I had at that time was in buying a camcorder to make sure there was a visible history of my wife preserved for my kids. Everything in life was now do different, viewed through tainted eyes."

Have you become involved in Shirley's care to the extent that the helplessness has lessened at all?

"No, my wife has taken full responsibility for her rehabilitation and health. In the beginning you try to be superman and do it all. This eventually turns to burn out, then resentment for feeling that you're not appreciated. That is from my perspective. Remember, at that time [in the first few years after diagnosis] Shirl was coping with survival.

"[As the financial burden lifted and] as her health stabilized so did our relationship, and helplessness faded away. Even as her condition worsened and she was listed for transplant, time has replaced helplessness with perspective and hope for the future."

How has living with this chronic illness changed your relationship?

"Since relationships ebb and flow through normal marriages, who's to say where we would be right now? It took about four years before we could actually talk about how we each felt about the effects of the disease on a personal level. In the early years we both talked about many things as long as they were not about how we felt towards Alpha-1. Then we finally started talking about it one night as we returned from shopping for groceries... I think you reach a point where you understand it's the disease [that is bad], not the person.

"Actually, as I think about it, there were times where she needed me to be there and other times when I felt like I should be there but was not wanted. It was a feeling of disconnection, or feeling unwanted because I was not considered as part of the "Alpha community." People identify with others who are the same. No matter how much I can imagine what it is like to be the one with the disease, I can't experience it.

"The same is true for the Alpha's. The person with the disease has a hard time understanding the fears and emotions of knowing you will eventually lose someone you love dearly. At Alpha conferences often the well spouses are drawn to each other and discuss their plight, while the Alpha's discuss medications and new research with each other. Of course it is more socially acceptable for the ill person to discuss those things than well spouses criticizing their ill spouses in public. The public expects well spouses to be fine upstanding citizens who would never criticize a loved one. The well spouse is expected to be there, strong, reassuring, and never complain.

"The first question a friend or relative asks is, 'How is Shirley?'... My friends have learned the best thing is honesty. Ask me direct questions, but expect real answers. Sometimes all a well spouse needs is someone to listen. We aren't necessarily expecting advice and sometimes a good cry is what we need. Ask about us as you would ask a person in a normal situation. Not everything experienced is disease related. And don't be taken aback by humor. It's my best defense against this disease. My friends can laugh with me when I tell them about Shirley's oxygen hose getting caught in my toes. They know how hard it was for me to learn to stick a needle in my wife's arm and they know my pride in seeing her complete a cross-country bike ride.

"This disease has helped Shirley blossom into a person who people hold in high regard, and as a leader. It may be she feels if I am given any credit for support or sacrifice, it lessens the accomplishment that she has worked hard for. In fairness to her, she believes that her fight is of a larger magnitude. However, the fight is hers, mine, and our children's. Maybe my ego is just a bit bruised. It's easy to lose one's identity in these situations.

As far as household chores go, do you ever feel that Shirley does too little? Too much?

"Yes, and yes! ... It seems that the better she feels the less willing she is to help out. The worse she feels the more she does. I believe it's because when she is down she needs to reassure herself that she can still do things... The reality is that I know she would prefer to be healthy and able.

"But of course it's always easier to be pissed off about the little things until you remember that the inverse is that she could be gone soon and you have wasted time being angry over insignificant little things. But, it still happens."

What have your children's reactions been to Shirley's diagnosis and her limitations?

"Now the kids, on the other hand, seem to cope better. They fill their party balloons with oxygen from the oxygen concentrator, roll on the IV pole, and know that Mom races bikes (see Shirley's interview) for a living. We don't live a bad life, just have a different life."

Is your house a bit of a circus sometimes? Where do your kids get that "roll with the punches" attitude?

Yes, it can be a circus, but it was always like that... Our kids probably get their attitude from both of us. Except in the early years of diagnosis we never have felt defeated. They also all possess our stubborn streak! I worry less and think that they have learned some positive things from this. This may help shape them in the future more than anything they ever will learn from school.

Author's note: Dave and Shirley separated shortly after these interviews. Many thanks to Dave and Shirley for their openness in sharing this part of their life. Acknowledgment goes as well to their children, Matt, Josh, Scott, Nick, and

Kate. May they always possess compassion and understanding, comfort and joy.

Todd's Story

Mary Pierce's (see Mary's story) husband, Todd, also has some insight on his role as well spouse and their experience with Alpha-1. Todd has been directly involved with Mary's battle to regain and maintain her health. Although they make a good team, he is far less well known, quietly working from the sidelines and researching. After finding recently that Todd had checked on something, Mary seemed confounded. Todd says, "I finally asked her, after all these years, if she should really be surprised."

Todd, did you ever feel sorry for Mary?

"Well, one of us should and she doesn't seem to take the time to. I can say that I spend lots more time on empathy than sympathy."

Were you ever angry?

"No."

Did you ever wonder, "Why us?"

"I was raised as a Norwegian. We don't expect much and what we do expect isn't pretty.... Mary was raised in the midst of continuing medical calamities so maybe she is not as frightened as one who is innocent of such things."

How has the illness changed your relationship? I sense that you have a tremendously deep admiration for Mary.

"Until she got sick I didn't think I ever did much without her. Now I will go out and shoot, ride, whatever, alone. It is not a big thing, though, and I don't think much has changed. I have never been bored by my own company. I do have a deep respect for Mary and the things she has done and for the admirable person she is."

Do you think this whole ordeal has strengthened your relationship?

"No, I think I expected this kind of fiber from her from the very start. I don't know that the relationship has changed any more than confirming what I knew was there has been proven out. What first attracted me to Mary was that she seemed very unafraid."

Why do you think that people sometimes avoid talking directly about a disease?

"I think if it is looked straight on it would be too easy to just start blubbering and the time for that is when the fight is lost...I try to not speak of it much as a matter of policy lest it seem to take even more of our lives. We...just cover what we need to. When we've been given some bad news, instead of giving Mary a hug and probably having a cry, I might mention some of the hopeful stuff I knew she had seen and let the subject drop. Brutal?... Is this indirect way of doing things more stressful than just brutally facing them down? I don't know. At the end of the day the only thing I can be certain of is that it is a brutal situation so there will be some brutality anyway. And that any extra stress can be put to good use... Please understand that I make no claims as to the wisdom or efficacy of the way I have tried to manage things. In fact I wonder if I may have been brutal. I just am not wise enough to handle it differently."

Did you ever think, "If we don't talk about it, maybe it will go away?"

"No, that has never been part of it... We talk about it but in a very deliberately unstructured fashion. We nibble around the edges. But I have to say that from the very first I absolutely knew she would come through in spite of the odds, which at that time were zero percent. Maybe that is denial."

No, I think that might be called not accepting defeat.

Is there a fear factor?

"Oh, you bet! But fear / stress has developed to motivate any animal out of a tight situation. It has a purpose."

This disease has taken up a big chunk of your lives. Is there ever a time when you and / or Mary forget about it altogether, if only for a moment, or is it always somewhere on your minds?

"Though I have tried to not let it seem that this is a consuming thing, in fact, it is. It can be pervasive and even insidious. I think this is typical of at least some others. It is that, since the future is so tenuous, it is hard to make plans ahead. I think Mary handles this better than I do. Maybe since she must carefully schedule her life, she is forced to. For myself, anything past a very few days hence falls into the category of the impossibly distant future.

"For example, an annual family gathering is coming up in a few weeks. This is a very big deal for us. It is a time when I can laugh and unwind among good friends who are family. My son repeatedly asked at this gathering last year, 'Who are you, and what have you done with my father?'

"We had a grand time. Last year Mary was on the phone with a friend who heard laughter coming from the house. This friend thought it remarkable. She was amazed to hear a laugh. I didn't appreciate that it had gotten that bad. I used to be thought of as happy-go-lucky. Now here we are only a few weeks away and I will only believe [we are going] about the time that I pack my bags... My head is so full of all the thousand calamities that could befall before then that it seems very far off... I have not been able to take myself in hand to fight it. This has been the case since Mary was diagnosed... To put on rose-colored glasses and pretend that the future will arrive uneventfully would absolutely be living in a fools' paradise."

Do you ever feel like you've lost your identity? Just being in the shadows as Mary's husband?

"I frequently introduce myself in Alpha groups as 'Mr. Mary Pierce.' In that group it is precisely who I am. I am well aware that in a medical situation all attention is properly upon the one who is bleeding. In my own element I can hold my head up as I am one of the best at what I do. Unfortunately, what I do is monumentally prosaic and uninteresting."

How did you know what you should do for Mary and what she should have done on her own?

"One does what the person with the disease cannot or should not do. But it is terribly important that the sick person should be allowed, *encouraged,* to do all they can. If they don't do all they can their self worth will vanish. Even if they were a couch potato before, it is important that the person [with CLD] does all they can, because now they *want* to do things. We got Mary a bell that she kept beside her when she could no longer call out. When I heard the bell I came right away knowing that she needed help with something. She never, ever, rang it without cause, and I never let it slide thinking maybe she was crying wolf.

"At that time we were aware of some patients who became the 'dolls' of the caregiver. The patient was bathed and doted upon generally, both before and after transplant. The outcomes I am familiar with were uniformly poor and even tragic.

Shirley's Story

When Shirley St. Cyr first received the diagnosis of Al-pha-1 Antitrypsin Deficiency she felt she might as well have been given a death sentence. At the time of her diagnosis, little hope was given to patients with the disease. Then only 29 years old, Shirley was one of the youngest known lung-affected Alpha patients in the United States (children with Alpha-1 are liver-affected and have transplants early in childhood). Since then, she has continuously worked to raise awareness for Alpha-1 by cycling on various bicycling treks throughout the country. In August 1998 Shirley completed a 48-day bicycle ride across the United States, probably being the first person ever to cycle across the U.S. with lung disease severe enough to require oxygen all the way. Here are some of her thoughts about being the "cared-for" person with Chronic Lung Disease.

How did you react to the diagnosis?

"At first I just slept. It was almost like a blackout, almost as if I were in a coma. This started in November and didn't really clear until late February. Dave thought I was depressed. But I was emaciated and I was exhausted. I hadn't realized I was as sick as I was. [Following diagnosis] I believe my body was trying to conserve any and all reserve I had to just perform the vital functions and to protect my brain from the effects of starvation and oxygen deprivation. I can't prove it, but I believe I could possibly have decided then that I would die, and therefore I would have. I just *decided* to fight. It could have gone either way. Fight or die."

How did the diagnosis change you?

"Once I came out of the sleep I felt that I no longer had the *choice* to work at my job as a nurse or to stay home. But I wasn't going to stand for that loss of independence. I thought, 'I'm going to beat this. I'm going to see the twins start kindergarten.' As far as getting better was concerned I knew that nobody else could do it for me. I had to do this myself. Although people could show their support, they could not participate in that aspect of it. I had always been a high achiever, but I became even more determined."

Did you ever feel helpless?

"Yes, at first. There wasn't a whole lot of hope. I had been given a death sentence. I felt helpless *and* hopeless."

Were you angry?

"No, not at the disease. I was angry with others' reactions toward me. I had a lung disease, not a mental disease. The diagnosis should not have changed their opinions of me as a person, but it did – overnight. I had always been considered as independent, headstrong, ambitious. Positive qualities. After diagnosis I was looked at as stubborn and pigheaded. Very negative."

What about acceptance? Was it difficult for you to accept the fact that you had this chronic disease? Did it take you a long time?

"I sought education and support almost since day one. I began going to Alpha meetings right away. But it wasn't real to me at the meetings. The people there were in their 50's. I was so young. I didn't know there was any solution until I met Mary [Pierce]."

What about the logistics of everyday living? How does the well spouse or caregiver know for sure who should do what when daily routines have had to change?

"It depends on how motivated the sick person is. Allow them to do all they can do and want to do. If the caregiver wants to be helpful, they should do the things they know the patient should *not* do, the things that would be harmful for them to do. It does get to the point after a while that the sick one will realize they can't do some things."

What would you like to see done differently?

"Medically, the way the diagnosis is handed out. There should be more education and information available at that time, rather than, 'You're going to die in five years.' I would also liked to have seen more involvement from Dave. Families need to be better educated, not merely with the scientific explanations, but with understanding the disease as it affects the whole person."

What do you feel the person with Chronic Lung Disease needs most from their caregiver / well spouse?

"Know and *understand* that when the person is stable, the impact [the degree of disability] depends on their level of disease. If they need a nap, don't make them feel like a bum. Know that they might not be able to get up in the morning and be out the door in an hour. We move slowly, especially in the first part of our day.

"Most of all, allow us the freedom, the independence, to make choices regarding our own health. Having a diagnosis of Chronic Lung disease may be black and white to anyone who doesn't have it, but it can cause us to feel better or worse day to day, minute to minute. It's a highly variable illness. We [the diagnosed] don't *decide* to be well or sick, we live by the ability or the inability to breathe."

Shirley St. Cyr and Mary Pierce in Washington, D.C. at the end of the
GTE Big Ride Across America

Resources for the Caregiver

www.thoracic.org/ca.html
Information on "Living With and Caring for Persons with Chronic Lung Disease"
202 Fashion Lane
Suite 219
Tustin, CA. 92780-3320
(714) 730-1944

www.caressentials.com
Care Essentials. Dedicated to supporting those who provide care for patients of serious/terminal illness.

www.wellspouse.org
Well Spouse Foundation
30 East 40th St.
Suite PH
New York, NY 10016
(212) 685-8815

Section Seven

Things That Help

"You don't give up. You just fight.
With a rehabilitation program it gets better."
--Stella Surko, Hamtramck, MI

Exercise? Are You Kidding?
Pulmonary Rehabilitation

Exercise as a treatment for shortness of breath? For the person struggling with breathlessness due to emphysema, chronic bronchitis, asthma, or other chronic lung disease, exercising might seem impossible. But comprehensive Pulmonary Rehab is becoming increasingly recognized as the gold standard of treatment for many of these disorders.

What kind of results can you expect from a Pulmonary Rehab Program?

✓ to increase your knowledge about your Chronic Lung Disease and how to manage it

✓ to improve your ability to take care of your overall health and breathing more effectively

✓ to have fewer emergency room visits and hospital admissions due to breathing problems

✓ to improve your physical conditioning, stamina, and flexibility

✓ to learn how to better cope with Chronic Lung Disease

✓ to learn how to feel less anxious and depressed about your breathing

✓ to have fun while finding friendship and support, knowing that you're not alone!

212

What do I need to do to start Pulmonary Rehab?

- Talk to your doctor. You need a physician's OK to begin a program.

- Be ready to work with your Pulmonary Rehab staff to find out what you can do to help yourself. Others can guide and support you, but nobody can do it for you. Once you recognize this you're on your way to a life of better living and better breathing!

Bill's Story

"The more I exercise, even though it tires me, the better I feel."
Clarence E. Ashley

Bill Horden wrote for and championed the cause of COPD'ers everywhere. His original website, which had been visited more than 20,000 times, contained among other things, his article "A COPD Survival Guide." The Survival Guide has been distributed in many countries and republished in Australia and Norway. For many years following his diagnosis Bill exercised at least five days a week and maintained correspondence with an online support group as well as the Cheshire Forum for Chronic Lung Disease. Bill's work is now carried on by his son Chip on the COPD International website. The following are Bill's words.

"I am now 71, have had "end stage" emphysema / COPD for twelve years and been on oxygen, 24 / 7, for the last six. I have been through an excellent pulmonary rehabilitation program.

"Along the way I have developed right-side coronary problems that required an AV node ablation, implantation of a pacemaker, and new drugs. I recently underwent cardioversion (to slow the atrial fibrillation)

214

but that failed, so I'm now on yet another new drug. (All this is pertinent only because the COPD is the root cause of my coronary problem.) In December 1999 I was diagnosed with lung cancer and underwent 30 radiation treatments for that annoyance. We think it was successful.

"I was 63 years old when I was, again, advised by my family doctor, 'Quit smoking.' Oh, I'd been treated with theophylline [one of the oldest breathing medicines, a pill you swallow] for seven years because of my asthma and chronic bronchitis, and had heard the 'stop smoking' thing for all that time but, except for a dozen half-hearted attempts, had quite successfully failed to quit.

"I moved from Texas to California in 1993, seeing a new family doctor, and it was he who pronounced the COPD / emphysema diagnosis. He also administered another quit smoking advice as well as several inhalers, and instructions to slow down and take things easy. His treatment plan was so unproductive that in 1995 I told this family doctor, who had since become the primary care physician in my HMO, that two years of care had brought absolutely no improvement to my condition. I had, in fact, declined to the point where I was not only unable to work, but couldn't do household chores, gardening, or anything but read or watch TV.

"I can't even take a shower without assistance," I said. I asked, "Shouldn't I be seeing a Pulmonologist?" He said he supposed it might be a good idea.

"It took only one visit to this lung specialist to determine that I needed supplemental oxygen and just one phone call for his nurse to arrange it. The equipment, tubing, and portable tanks were delivered the next day and I was instructed to use the oxygen 24 hours a day, seven days a week. But, still, I had yet to receive an explanation of the disease called 'COPD.'

"(This boring chronology is provided because, since that time, I have corresponded with thousands of others with COPD and have found that eighty or ninety percent of them were introduced to their disease in exactly the same manner.)

"After dutifully using oxygen, 24/7, for two months, I called the pulmonologist and said, 'I feel no better, and this hose-in-the-nose is a pain in the backside. In fact, I can't even walk thirty feet to the bathroom without gasping for breath.' His response was to tell me that St. Jude Medical Center, in Fullerton, CA, was starting a rehab / wellness program and he would try to get me into it. His secretary called an hour later, gave me the name of a doctor associated with the program, and an appointment time for the very next day. She also sent along her personal wish that I might be accepted (and that my insurance would pay).

"I kept the Thursday appointment, was approved by the physician, and instructed to report at 9:00 am, Monday, for Session One. This doctor was sure the rehab would help, and that my HMO could be persuaded to pay.

"It has occurred to me, from time to time, that it was so very lucky that I had little time over that weekend, to think about 'Pulmonary Rehabilitation,' and that, having had no computer, I had no ready way to research the subject. Had it sunk into my brain that some Pulmonary Therapists were actually going to require me, who couldn't do a thing without help, to *exercise*, and that I would soon be able to shop, prepare meals, or play with my grandchildren, well, I'd have known it *couldn't work*.

"I had tried, you know, really tried to do things, but I was falling apart. Literally falling apart! How could exercise help? I'm not stupid, you know! In my ignorance, or because the doctor had been so calmly persuasive, I dutifully showed up Monday, anticipating the miracles they would perform.

"As I went through the next eight weeks, three days a week, I found miracles I never expected. The greatest one being that a dedicated doctor and his staff of equally committed therapists could help a totally disparate group of pulmonary patients learn how to manage their diseases and, in so doing, return to them some control of their lives, restore lost hope, and improve the quality of their lives. I saw us learning how, after the course was completed, we could continue to exercise, manage our medications, communicate with our doctors, and slow the progress of our maladies.

"I also witnessed the birth of a support group. I witnessed total strangers develop bonds that helped each other to work harder during exercise sessions, laugh at our clumsiness, coach a partner, and become lifelong friends; sharing problems, trials, and victories others would, hopefully, never know.

"I can't say, positively, that pulmonary rehab saved my life, but I can say that it gave me a better, longer, richer life.

Nick's Story

"I thank the good Lord for every day he gives me to help lighten someone else's life, and help them in any small way I am able."
Lois Felinski, Warren, MI

A self-described "farm boy" Nick Wilkinson grew up during the depression in rural West Michigan and lived there almost all his life. After serving in the Air Force in World War II as a control tower operator in Berlin, he returned home, got married and became the father of four children. Settling down to civilian life, Nick worked in the farm implement business, eventually owning a share in his family's farm equipment company. From time to time Nick noticed that some things in his environment such as dust, mold, and humidity caused his breathing to feel "tight." All the while he smoked cigarettes. Like so many people Nick smoked for a long time and never thought it would catch up with him. Here is his story about how Pulmonary Rehab gave him help and hope.

It was a warm summer night and Nick had a problem. He was having a lot of trouble breathing and didn't know what to do. He was nearing the point of panic.

218

"What's happening to me?" he wondered. "Am I going to die?"

It was taking all Nick had to take in each breath. He had a horrible, suffocating feeling, and was wondering if each breath would be his last.

Nick was rushed by ambulance to the hospital emergency room. There he had X-rays, breathing treatments, and other medications as well as arterial blood gases (ABG's), a test that shows the oxygen level in the blood. Nick's ABG's revealed a low oxygen level, a real wake up call. The doctor working in the emergency room that night warned Nick that if he didn't give up smoking, he would soon need to wear supplemental oxygen.

The infection that had made his breathing worse that terrible night eventually went away, but the process of facing up to the damage done to his lungs from years of smoking had just begun.

Although Nick got past that frightening emergency episode and was able to quit smoking, his breathing over the next few years was self-described as "a struggle" at best. He seemed to be doing less, but becoming short of breath and tired more quickly. Nick's breathing was getting worse and worse. This downward slide in his activity level left him to wonder what was in his future. There were still things he wanted to do, things to enjoy. Having been a widower, Nick now found wonderful companionship with his second wife, Blanche. But if he couldn't breathe and couldn't move, what would happen to him from here on? Would Nick soon be spending his days just sitting in his chair, unable to do much of anything? These changes prompted Blanche, also, to worry about what would happen to her husband, a man who had been so strong and healthy, who she now saw struggling so hard just to breathe.

Some time after his trip to the emergency room, Nick was receiving therapy for a problem with his shoulder. The

Physical Therapist told him about Pulmonary Rehab. Nick asked his internal medicine doctor about it and was referred to a Pulmonary Rehabilitation program.

When Nick walked into the Pulmonary Rehab department at age 71, the staff saw first, a man who was definitely struggling to breathe. Next, they saw Nick as a handsome man, a charmer, with a bit of a mischievous twinkle in his eye. It was easy to notice his brightly colored suspenders, as well as his look of concern. At this initial evaluation, the first step of a Pulmonary Rehab program, he told the staff softly, **"My doctor thinks this program will help, and my wife wants me to come, but I don't know if there's anything you people can do to help me."**

As Nick began participating in the program, he remained skeptical. Back then he thought his inhalers were doing him more harm than good, he didn't believe that a pulse oximeter (a device the staff used to check oxygen saturation) really worked, and couldn't imagine how pursed-lip breathing could help. He questioned everything, but in a good-natured way. Boy, did the Pulmonary Rehab staff have their work cut out for them!

With Blanche at his side, Nick drove 25 miles one way twice a week (in the West Michigan winter!) to participate in exercise and education. Gradually Nick's exercise capacity increased along with his confidence in what was being taught to him by the staff. He felt so much better and had more control over his breathing; rather than feeling as if his breathing had control over him. Indeed, Nick was reaping the rewards of his hard work, continuing commitment, and positive attitude. This success made him a firm believer in the value of Pulmonary Rehab.

"Before this program, I didn't know *what* to do to help myself. But here I learned how to use my inhalers, and that they really do work. I've also learned to live with my lung condition."

"A big part of it is that he's learned to cope," added Blanche.

Before coming to the program Nick didn't know how to avoid breathing troublemakers or how to watch for the early warning signs of a bad episode.

"I've learned how to think ahead and not get myself into these circumstances. It's also helped a lot to work with my doctor and be able to ask questions of him and the staff here. And I've learned that exercise helps. Pulmonary Rehab has definitely been worth the time and effort. It really has."

Nick went on to continue in the maintenance phase of Pulmonary Rehab, faithfully attending exercise every week while having fun and making new friends in class. A goal of his, as a result of participating in the program, was to start bowling again, which he did. Nick also rediscovered the joy of driving his tractor and traveling with Blanche. Knowing how much participating in Pulmonary Rehab had helped him to breathe better, feel better, *live* better, Nick, a former skeptic, became one of the program's biggest promoters. He encouraged friends and acquaintances afflicted with COPD to live better by joining Pulmonary Rehab.

Often after exercise class Nick would pause a few minutes to talk privately with staff. He would put his hand on a staff member's shoulder, sincerely and emotionally saying, "You people have helped me so much. I just want to see others have the chance to improve like I have."

Nick Wilkinson on his tractor

I love Pulmonary Rehab
Number One: Get involved!
Special instructors
People who encourage each other
It makes me feel healthy
Really having fun
Attitude makes the difference
Total dedication
It has made me a believer. Exercise works!
Ongoing participation keeps me strong
Never give up!

This acrostic poem was compiled by the
Pulmonary Rehab participants
of Holland Community Hospital,
March 1999

How to find a program

Call your local hospital and ask if they have a Pulmonary Rehab program. If they don't, ask where the nearest program is located. If they don't know, contact the American Association for Cardiovascular and Pulmonary Rehabilitiation (AACVPR) www.aacvpr.org or call 1-608-831-6989.

What will it be like?

"I'm kind of scared. What will they make me do in Pulmonary Rehab?"

Six minute walk. You might walk with a therapist or nurse while having your oxygen monitored. Don't worry. They only count the distance you cover. If you walk for one minute and rest for five, that's alright. This is just a start.

Warm up stretches and strengthening. Each program varies. You might work with dowls, stretchy bands, or light weights.

Exercise equipment. Stationary bikes, bikes with moving arms, arm peddlers, rowing machines, recumbent steppers, and treadmills are just some of the equipment you might have the option to use. Remember, the staff at pulmonary rehab is used to working with people with shortness of breath. They'll help your exercise to be easy and fun.

You'll also attend classes which teach you about your lungs, medications, diet, special breathing techniques, ways to relax, and ways to cope with shortness of breath.

Thanksgiving

It was the Tuesday before Thanksgiving; John walked into the Pulmonary Rehab gym, and then stopped. He told me he had something to tell the class and asked if he could have a few minutes for that.

"Sure, that's fine. What is it?"

"Something I want to share with them. You'll see."

The members of the eleven o'clock class sat together, waiting for exercise to start. John slowly stood, white folded paper in hand and shared with the group, this, his thoughts on Thanksgiving.

I was reminded one recent Sunday morning that I should try to be thankful for adversity and challenges in my life. I have a pulmonary problem. How can I possibly be *thankful* for this breathing challenge?

I thought of my Pulmonary Rehab class at Holland Community Hospital. The need for discipline and exercise in breathing brought me into this class and in contact with its several leaders and classmates. It is these people that give to me my reason for thanksgiving. Because of them my life is fuller, more enriched. But how is this possible? I'll tell you.

I had some concern about a grandson. Jane, a respiratory therapist, has teenagers herself. She assured me not to be discouraged. "It will all work out alright," she said. Without her assurance, worry would have eaten away at me. I am thankful for Jane. I am thankful for acceptance and assurance.

Lynda, a nurse, is concerned about areas of my health other than pulmonary. She shows concern about my heart and fluid balance, and sometimes insists I contact my internist. I am thankful for Lynda. I am thankful for vigilant health care professionals.

Ruth always asks, "How are you feeling today, John?" If she didn't ask, I wouldn't know that someone really cares. I am thankful for Ruth. I am thankful for sincere concern.

Can my adversity be met and overcome? I know it can! Bud has shown this to me by his perseverance through a lung transplant. It may take months or years, but improvement is possible. I am thankful for Bud. I am thankful for witnessing the miracle of organ donation and for perseverance in the face of overwhelming odds.

Dave has a caustic wit that cheers me up. Without him I might not know that merriness can be so close at hand. With Dave in the class, I can laugh. I am thankful for Dave. I am thankful for laughter.

Bernie and Shirley remind me that God is still on the throne. I need to visit with them while exercising. They reassure me in a spiritual way. If I did not have this breathing problem I would not be in rehab and would miss out on the conversations we have. Bernie and Shirley are a beautiful couple. I am thankful for them. I am thankful for lasting faith.

Glenn and I have mutual friends. He keeps me posted on their whereabouts. Without his sharing in rehab, who would keep me in touch? I am thankful for Glenn. I am thankful for connectedness.

One of my rehab classmates is a man from Cambodia. Om reminds me that life reaches past my background and around the world. Although he understands little English, Om always has a bright and cheerful smile for me. My life would be less without him. I am thankful for Om. I am thankful for smiles.

Mitzi shares with me her love and knowledge of classical music. She also communicates her concern about world events. Mitzi is a serious conversationalist. She makes me think. I am thankful for Mitzi. I am thankful for a new friend with sharp intellect.

For all the others in the class who inspire me by their determination, and for the staff members who help me, I am thankful. So now, because of my breathing problem, my life has become enriched. I have found joy and contentment in the midst of adversity. I am thankful for my pulmonary struggle. And I am thankful for the richness it brings.

John M. Smith

Taking a break at Pulmonary Rehab
(left to right) Om Koeun, Jane Martin, CRT, John Smith,
Lynda Schipper, RN, Beth Willis, EP

"Gratitude unlocks the fullness of life. It turns what we have into enough, and more. It turns denial into acceptance, chaos to order, confusion to clarity. It can turn a meal into a feast, a house into a home, a stranger into a friend. Gratitude makes sense of our past, brings peace for today, and creates a vision for tomorrow."

Melody Beattie
Writer

My Buddy, My Shadow, My Oxygen

"You are not alone."

Many people with Chronic Lung disease dread even the thought of going on oxygen. They may feel like when that happens, it is the beginning of the end, that their life as they've known it has ended; that they will be forever tethered to that tank by the hose.

What may be difficult to realize but is indeed a fact, is that using oxygen (O_2) as prescribed will help you to have more freedom than if you didn't use it. If you can walk farther with less shortness of breath, you'd rather do that, wouldn't you? Oxygen can help. Oxygen helps your heart and your lungs so they don't have to work so hard. That's a lot less stress, less "wear and tear" on your body, therefore allowing your body's systems to do their jobs nourished with enough oxygen to keep everything going for as long as possible. The using of oxygen as directed by a qualified physician can lengthen your life!

Mary Pierce says, "For me, going on oxygen was hard. There was some of the 'this is it' feeling, because if I'm needing oxygen, I'm going downhill. I suppose underneath it all was the fact that, for me, it meant that

I was closer to the end. The hose itself was so ugly. All the emphysema books, the pictures of older people, I resented that. I didn't like that at all. As far as going out, wearing my oxygen in public, I felt that others looked at me with fear, dislike, judgment. Guilt again. 'She's got emphysema. She smoked. She's stupid.' Just reinforcing what I believed."

When asked if she felt as if she were looked upon differently because she was wearing oxygen, Mary's reply was, "That patronizing does happen. You know, you can walk into a restaurant with crutches, or a cane, or be in a wheelchair. But, you know... that oxygen hose, it is totally different. Lung disease is not considered a disability by the general public. People see you and think, 'You look OK. What's wrong with you, why don't you move faster?'"

Others don't have such a big struggle with accepting that they'll have to use supplemental oxygen. They may be further along in the stages of acceptance. Herk Lake, and his wife, Eleanor, just accepted it. "Now he needs oxygen. I guess that's what we need to do," says Eleanor as she recalls their experience.

A participant in our Pulmonary Rehab program states, "Hey, I need it [my oxygen] to breathe. If somebody doesn't like it, that's their problem."

Some take a humorous approach. Jane Gillette has some advice:

"When the waiter sees the O$_2$ and asks whomever you are with, 'And what will *she* have?' (They assume even the family dog or a two-year-old could make a better decision!) That's when you tell them you still complete the New York Times crossword puzzle... in ink ... and then place your order."

Patrick Dooley, a member of the COPD internet support group shares his story.

"I have severe emphysema and I am on oxygen full time. I use the concentrator at home. I use the Bi-Pap [non-invasive ventilator] at night with oxygen, and use my little portable oxygen unit when I'm out and about. I still drive my touring motorcycle during the summer with my portable oxygen in a backpack. I carry a spare oxygen tank in one of the 'suitcases' and my portable nebulizer in the 'trunk'. Can't drive as far or as long as I used to, but as long as it is still fun, I intend to continue to ride. I live in the state of Oregon and in the woods. There is nothing like driving down the road that parallels a creek and down to the mighty Rogue River to get to Grant's Pass to do some errands. I might even stop along the way to do a nebulizer treatment down by a creek. Then, to save time and energy, I come back home via the Interstate. (Boring!!)"

Patrick Dooley with his motorcycle and oxygen

"Sure, using oxygen can be a hassle. It takes time to get used to be 'chained' to a machine at home. The hose catches on the corners, kitchen knobs and can change the position of the ears on one's head!! It can be a hassle to have in the shower, especially when it's time to wash the hair and face. *But one gets through it.* And eventually one becomes used to it. Just like getting used to wearing a pair of glasses, wearing oxygen is simply a tool to make one's life either easier or enable one to function with less shortness of breath. And that's where a portable oxygen unit can make a difference as it makes one keep the freedom to come and go and function out in the 'real' world. Even when needing supplemental oxygen one can have a near normal life!!"

Frequently Asked Questions and Some Myths Regarding Oxygen Therapy

by Dr. Steven Kraker, MD

1.) I am so short of breath. Why can't I have oxygen? or, I am not short of breath, doctor, why must I use the oxygen?

Believe it or not, in many cases you really cannot tell when you need or don't need oxygen. Many things contribute to shortness of breath, and though it is commonly believed by the lay person that shortness of breath means you need oxygen, that is not always the case. The converse is also true. Patients with significant lung disease who have chronically low blood oxygen levels sometimes refuse to use oxygen because they "don't feel short of breath." For accurate assessment of who needs oxygen and who doesn't we must rely on measured blood levels. This is done directly on blood drawn through a needle from an artery or indirectly by a simple device called an oximeter, which can accurately measure your blood oxygen level through your finger or your ear lobe. There are criteria that doctors use to determine who does and does not need oxygen, whether that be part time or 24 hours daily. These criteria are well established in the medical literature and are also adhered to by insurance companies in determine whether they will pay for prescribed oxygen. You can be quite short of breath and yet have an entirely normal blood oxygen level. In that case all of the oxygen we could possibly give is not going to affect your shortness of breath. There are other factors involved in that situation which must be treated in order to improve your shortness of breath.

Likewise, even patients who are not short of breath but yet have low blood oxygen levels can benefit from oxygen therapy in terms of quality of life and better functioning of important organs such as the brain, the heart, and the kidneys. In order to know whether you need oxygen or not your doctor needs to do some testing. If the testing does not indicate the need for oxygen, then attention needs to be focused on other contributing causes for your shortness of breath. Even though you may not qualify for oxygen at one time, it may be necessary to follow up your blood oxygen levels periodically (every 6 to 12 months) to determine if at some point in the future you may require oxygen therapy.

2.) If I start on oxygen now, won't I get addicted to it?

No, this is a myth. We have all essentially been "addicted" to oxygen since birth. We can't live without it. The air we breathe is approximately 21% oxygen. When a patient is started on supplemental oxygen they are often put on something in the range of 24 to 30% oxygen, so it is just a little more than is in the usual air you breathe. Using supplemental oxygen does not make you dependent on it anymore than you have already been dependent on it since your first breath. It is just that with lung disease you may need a little bit more oxygen going into your lungs in order to get an adequate amount through your diseased lungs into your blood stream.

Using supplemental oxygen does not result in increasing demand for oxygen. The increased need is simply related to the progression of your underlying lung disease. Often patients who need oxygen find that as years go by and their lung disease gradually worsens that it takes more oxygen to get the same blood level. This is not because they were started on supplemental oxygen. It is merely because the disease has progressed (as is the natural course of many lung diseases). Often times patients feel that oxygen may be addictive because once they are started on supplemental oxygen they "can never get off it." That is not because they have used the oxygen. It is just, again, related to their underlying disease. If the underlying lung disease is significant enough that oxygen is required in the first place, oxygen is likely going to always be required.

Sometimes, when people are right on the verge of needing oxygen, but not quite needing it on an everyday basis, they may come to need oxygen temporarily during an acute illness. This is something that can happen when a person is near the need for continuous oxygen therapy and with an acute illness they will be stressed enough to require oxygen temporarily. Then after recovery their oxygen level may be back up and they can come off oxygen again. Sometimes an acute illness will be the last straw that causes you to need supplemental oxygen from that point on.

If your doctor feels you need to use oxygen, you should use it without fear of it causing dependence. Studies show that if you meet the criteria for needing oxygen and use it according to your doctor's prescription that you will survive better and longer than a similar patient with a similar disease who chooses not to use oxygen.

3.) Can I use my oxygen just when I am in the privacy of my own home and not when I go out shopping or to the movies or out to dinner?

Using oxygen is sometimes inconvenient or embarrassing for patients and this leads to the temptation to "use it only when I need it." Again I would refer you to what we covered above and that is that you really can't tell when you need oxygen and when you don't unless your blood oxygen levels are being measured. Studies show that if you meet the criteria for continuous oxygen use, using it less than 18 hours a day is probably equivalent to using none at all. If your doctor prescribes 24 hour daily oxygen therapy you should try to use it as close to 24 hours a day as practical. Of course there are times you may need to take it off, when you shave or put on make-up or do other daily hygiene. This is not harmful for short periods of time. If you have any questions about this, it is a good idea to go over them with your doctor, pulmonary rehabilitation nurse, or respiratory therapist.

Occasionally patients need oxygen only at night while asleep. Other patients may only need oxygen part of the day, but usually this is with any type of exertion such as walking or getting out and doing errands, etc. If your doctor determines from testing that you do not need oxygen 24 hours a day, it will usually be necessary either at night during sleep or just when you are up and active, i.e. out doing errands or some of the activities we talked about above. Often in this situation the only time you really *don't* need supplemental oxygen is when you are sitting quietly resting at home reading a book or watching television. Human nature says that is the time you would like to be using your oxygen but ironically you really need it most when you are out and about.

4.) Can oxygen cure me?

No. Your oxygen does not treat your underlying lung disease. It just helps to fulfill needs that your diseased lungs cannot manage on their own. It is helping you to do a little better with what you have, but it can't improve your lung function. It is kind of like having to wear glasses because your eyes aren't entirely normal. Wearing glasses doesn't fix your eye problem. They just help your eyes to see better. If you take your glasses off, your eye problem is still there and you can't see very well. The same is true for your oxygen. It just helps you do a little better with the lungs you have. Your lungs are still the way they were. Your body cannot store oxygen, so if you take your oxygen off, your blood oxygen level will go back down again within minutes.

5.) I have heard there are different types of oxygen and different ways to administer oxygen. What is best for me?

Oxygen is oxygen and whether you use liquid oxygen tanks of gaseous oxygen or a device called an oxygen concentrator, it is individualized for each patient depending on their needs. You can get excellent treatment with supplemental oxygen by any of the types of oxygen just mentioned. Liquid oxygen is just gaseous oxygen compressed into a much smaller volume so that it becomes liquid. As it is allowed to escape from its container into your oxygen tubing it becomes gaseous oxygen the same as you would get from a simple oxygen tank. For patients who are more active and mobile, liquid oxygen can sometimes be a nice alternative because they can be out and about for a longer time using a smaller sized tank.

An oxygen concentrator is good for patients who are fairly sedentary and don't get out much. An oxygen concentrator takes oxygen from the air in a way similar to how a dehumidifier takes water from the air. Just like the water from your dehumidifier runs out through a hose into a drain, the oxygen from your oxygen concentrator runs through the tubing into your nose at a set flow rate prescribed by your doctor. The device runs on electricity in your home so you usually need to have some spare oxygen tanks in case there is a power outage.

Depending on your prescribed oxygen flow rate, a small portable tank may last you up to a few hours. Some patients like to get out more, sometimes for several hours at a time, and don't want to have to carry extra tanks with them. These patients might benefit from an oxygen conserving device. Usually these devices give you oxygen only every other, every third, or every fourth breath depending on how they are programmed. By extending the length of time you can go on a set amount of oxygen, you are actually using up less oxygen per minute. In some cases, this can be sufficient, but in other cases this is not adequate. Your doctor can test you to see if a conserving device is right for you.

The message is that oxygen is oxygen whether it is liquid, gaseous, or from a concentrator. The dose you need is whatever your doctor has determined is sufficient to maintain a normal blood oxygen level during your usual normal daily activities at home and away.

6.) I have heard there is something where you get oxygen through a little tube that goes through your neck into your windpipe. Is that for me?

What you are referring to is called transtracheal oxygen therapy. It is not a tracheostomy. It is a very small, soft, plastic tube that passes through the skin of your neck just below your Adam's apple and enters directly into your trachea or windpipe. This method of giving oxygen is used by patients who have had trouble with nasal or sinus problems from nasal oxygen or patients who get sores or ulcers from the oxygen tubing. It is also recommended for some patients who need so much oxygen that it is impractical to give it through the nose. You can get by on about half as much oxygen if it is given directly into the trachea as opposed to taking it into the nose. Some of the oxygen that goes into your nose unavoidably just escapes into the atmosphere.

The transtracheal oxygen catheter is not for all people who need oxygen. It does require some special care and you have to be able to do this care yourself on at least a daily basis, sometimes more. You still have to have a nasal cannula for oxygen to use when you are removing your transtracheal catheter and cleaning it, or for emergencies if your transtracheal catheter should come out. If you are wondering whether you are a candidate for transtracheal oxygen you should ask your doctor.

7.) I've heard that oxygen is dangerous. Too much can hurt you.

You should consider oxygen as a medication. Accordingly it should be treated like any other drug prescribed, that is, it should be used in appropriate doses. Just because some is good, it doesn't mean more oxygen is necessarily better. You should rely on the advice of your doctor who knows your particular case. Some lung diseases require a certain level of supplemental oxygen when the patient is at rest, but more oxygen is needed during times of exertion. Other lung diseases require a set amount of supplemental oxygen on a continuous basis, and increasing the dosage beyond the prescribed amount could be detrimental. You will have to discuss your own individual situation with your doctor to determine what is best for you.

Under some circumstances it can be detrimental to increase your own oxygen without consulting your doctor, just as if you increased your own heart medicine, blood pressure medicine, or diabetes medicine without consulting your doctor. Again, I think the best way to go about it is to think of your oxygen like another drug prescription and to follow the specific instructions very carefully just as you would with any of your other medicines.

Lung Support Groups for Patients and their Families

"Go to the meetings.
You'll find many people to encourage you."

When it comes to information about Pulmonary Support Groups, Jo-Von Tucker is the one to ask. Jo-Von very generously contributes her expertise in this chapter. What comes before, though, is a brief account of this courageous lady's life, in her own words, before and after her COPD diagnosis.

"I almost feel as though I have had two lives: one before diagnosis of COPD, and one after. The one before was busy, successful, and fulfilling in its way of achieving professional status and reputation. I loved my life of being able to consult in catalog marketing all over the world. And of course, there is the constant of my daughter and her family, still the thread that ties it all together, this life and the other.

"But A.D. (after diagnosis) my life took on new meaning... I truly believe that I was meant to write my book about lung disease and to do the work that I do now of coordinating the Cape COPD Support Group as well as writing and producing its monthly Newsletters.

"Beyond that, though, is the gift of compassion that living with this disease has brought me. I have new, deeper, more meaningful insight into the problems that people with any chronic illness face. I am more sensitive to the suffering of others. And I am compelled to help them in any way I can. Much of this is done now through my writing.

"Physically, my life consists of challenge after challenge. I continue to work each day in my own business, Clambake Celebrations... even on the inevitable days that find me sick and oh-so-fatigued. I am grateful to be able to do so, because it gives me a marching order to get up and out of bed every single morning. In addition to chronic obstructive pulmonary disease, I now fight a daily battle managing my diabetes, and worse yet, the curse of Post Polio Syndrome, which tears and pulls at the muscles of my body, inflicting me with pain and yet-more-fatigue.

"Still... at the end of the day, my biggest frustration is that I have either run out of time—or energy—or both. Like the White Rabbit in Through the Looking Glass, I rush from here to there, always fearing that I'll be late for that very important date.

"Successful and respected marketer? Yes, I was that. Driving entrepreneur? Yep, I am still that. Effective leader of a large support group for people with COPD? For sure, our 200+ membership must attest to that. But the most meaningful of all? It has to be my book, Courage and Information for Life With Chronic Obstructive Pulmonary Disease, and the number of lives it has touched; of patients, doctors, care givers, spouses and other family members of COPD-ers."

This chapter contains excellent and very comprehensive advice on starting and facilitating a pulmonary support group. Every reader may not necessarily have the resources available to provide this level of service to their group. However, I do strongly encourage you to either join an existing group, or consider organizing one, no matter how small or modest it may be.

The Role of Lung Support Groups for Patients and Family Members

by Jo-Von Tucker, Founder/Coordinator of the
Cape Cod COPD Support Group

Support groups for people with lung disease can provide an important foundation for learning to live with and manage the disease. There is *nothing* more reinforcing and comforting than being in a room full of people who know *exactly* how you feel! This is especially important to COPD patients, who may be embarrassed by their oxygen equipment, or intimidated by the general lack of knowledge of COPD and understanding by the public. This statement may also include loving spouses and conscientious care givers and friends, all of whom may sadly *misunderstand* the severe lifestyle compromises this debilitating illness causes for those most directly affected... the patient.

What better place for a lung patient to air his or her consuming questions and issues about life with a usually progressive, so-far incurable chronic illness? Where could a more receptive and empathetic audience be found to hear worries and doubts expressed that fully mirror their own? From whom could a newly diagnosed patient learn more about conserving precious energy; or how to properly use a spacer with their puffers; or how important physical rehabilitation is to their ability to maintain some quality of life?

In every support group there are certain members who are more effectively coping with their lung disease than others. These individuals, collectively or separately, serve as role models for the rest of the group. They set the pace, lead by example, and inspire by their very presence, the more devastated members in need of help and encouragement.

These "leaders" are the ones who completed the pulmonary rehabilitation courses in fine relative shape and condition. Usually they are the ones who attend *all* of the meetings, and many times they are the ones who volunteer for the various projects a group may have undertaken. They seem to suffer from fewer exacerbations, resulting in fewer hospital stays, as well. They are the consummate survivors who will provide the backbone (and the *raison d' etre)* for the entire group. Not coincidentally, they also make the best coordinators for lung support groups. A study conducted in the New York City area by lung support groups has proved that *patient-led (lay-led) support groups are by far the most successful ones.*[7]

But besides these highly motivated people, a meeting of any lung support group will also contain the regular folks who are frequently gripped by periods of depression, brought on by necessary compromises required by lung patients. These are people who frequently have no one else to talk with about how they are feeling. Many of them have learned most of what they know about obstructive or restrictive lung disease from attending the support group meetings, or from reading articles published in their respective newsletters.

Think about it, doctors today are under tremendous pressure from HMO's and hospitals, and other changing criteria of our contemporary medical profession. They don't have the time—or the inclination—to be the educator of patients. Most people, after a brief session with a pulmonologist, are turned out to fend for themselves in the scary world of lung

243

disease, scheduled to return only in six months or so for an even briefer checkup.

Pulmonary rehab courses provide wonderful education for patients, but after an eight-week session their overseeing responsibilities are over. Some rehab facilities offer a continuing maintenance program with more informal exercise, socialization and group support. However, it is important to find a good support group in your local area that meets regularly and produces an informative newsletter that allows a patient exposure to important educational information regarding their disease on an ongoing basis. It also subjects them to exposure to other lung patients who are managing their lives and their illness as effectively as possible, which provides encouragement to those around them.

✍ Different Kinds of Support Groups ✍

There are several kinds of support groups for lung disease: one type is pulmonary rehabilitation courses that offer support group participation sponsored by the hospital or rehab facility. Usually these groups can only be joined if the patient has completed the pulmonary rehab course that is offered. It may provide regular exercise classes or walking sessions for members, and/or the sponsorship of social gatherings. They are usually professionally led, many times by a pulmonary or rehab nurse.

The American Lung Association frequently is the sponsor for another type of lung support group that springs up in cities or towns close to the ALA regional or state offices. They may be referred to as Better Breathers Clubs. These groups are mostly lay-led, most often by COPD, asthma or lung cancer patients themselves. Their agendas vary, but the more successful ones offer monthly meetings that alternate between knowledgeable speakers on lung disease and interactive discussion formats, during which attendees are invited to bring up any issue regarding their concerns or experiences with lung illness for group participation.

It is important to get the backing and support of local pulmonary physicians, respiratory care therapists and oxygen providers, hospitals and rehabilitation facilities for any type of lung support group to survive. These professionals and organizations will prove to be a good source for new member referrals, and may help to support the group financially. They will also help to provide speakers for programs. The American Lung Association can also be a source of some of the funding for operations of a lung group. And they can also provide very good informational booklets on a variety of lung illnesses for distribution to members.

A third kind of support group is an online list, reachable over the Internet. These groups function like chat rooms (except that they are usually not live interaction). People who have registered and belong to the online group can tap into the list at any time of day or night via their computer, addressing a question or bringing up an issue to all who choose to participate at that time. A good question may elicit scores of responses via the online list. People are very willing to share their knowledge about an illness. If one member posts an answer that the other members consider inaccurate or incomplete, the group will quickly point out the errors in the communication.

The only drawback to an online support group is the fact that older people have generally been intimidated by the wizardry of the electronic medium, or may not have access to their own computer. But this situation is changing rapidly, as Senior Centers all over the country are offering courses on computers and their use, resulting in more and more of the elderly population having cyber-savvy. For some internet links to websites, please see "on-line resources" in the back of this book.

Support groups for people with lung disease should have a two-fold mission:

To provide information and education regarding lung illnesses and their management .

To provide a forum for lung patients from which to share their experiences and on which to build ongoing, emotionally supportive relationships and friendships.

Both areas of responsibility are important to members, their families and care givers. Support group meetings should be open to those family members if they wish to attend with the patient. They will learn about the disease just by listening, and it will lead to better understanding between patient and spouse or caregiver. Just like the patient, they will learn about the good days and bad days that are a part of COPD and other lung illnesses. They will better recognize the signs of exacerbation and acute breathing distress, and learn when to call for help and when to sit it out. They will also learn when to offer help to the patient, and when to let the affected person push their boundaries of activity and physical involvement.

Whether or not the spouses and caregivers choose to attend meetings, the role of the support group for patients remains an integral part of overall treatment and care. One of our founding members in the Cape COPD Support Group lay dying after a severe pneumonia infection. She chose to spend her last few minutes with her 3 sons at her side, telling them over and over again how much our support group had meant to her—how much it had helped her, how much better she understood the illness because of what the group had taught her, and how grateful she was for the friendships she had formed in the group. When one of her sons related her last words to me after she had passed on, it was very moving, and immensely rewarding.

This member had always attended the support group meetings alone. She was a widow, and none of her family members had ever visited our meetings. The group had given her life, even with the disease that she faced every day, new meaning and inspiration. She, in turn, had given back to the group. We all knew that we could count on her to be present unless she was very ill. She contributed passionately to our group discussions, and offered comfort to those members who were going through an especially rough time. Her New England sense of fairness and equality always assured us that she was listening intently and judging no one. And her suggestions for solutions were always realistic and achievable. Her last thoughts in this world were of the people in her support group.

➤ Lung Support Group Newsletters ➤

The promise, tone and character of a support group is truly carried by the newsletter it produces. I have found that a monthly newsletter, published to arrive about a week before the next scheduled meeting, serves to educate members and other recipients, and to remind them to attend the coming meeting.

We currently have a database of about 350 people who receive the mailing each month. It is made up of 185 full-fledged members of the group, with about 50 recipients who are COPD patients but who live too far away to attend meetings (one subscriber lives in Hawaii—a very long way from Cape Cod, Massachusetts). The rest go to professionals like pulmonary doctors, primary care physicians, respiratory care therapists, VNA's (Visiting Nurse Associations), Councils on Aging, etc. Additionally, we have some distribution of the newsletter in the offices and waiting rooms of pulmonologists in the area.

✒ Financial Support ✒

Most of the funding for our activities is provided by the members themselves. We suggest a donation of $24 per year, which includes the 12 newsletters. In the event that a prospective member cannot afford the suggested donation, we are amenable to accepting less, or even nothing. No one is ever turned away.

Even though the American Lung Association contributes $100 per month toward the expenses of publishing our newsletter, the cost to do so is about 3 times that amount, so we must have contributions from most members. The postage alone is about $68, with printing and paper costs running close to $200 each month. For those members who write us to ask to receive the newsletters, even though they may live far away from our group, we suggest a donation of $15 per person per year for the 12 issues.

Our monthly newsletter is written and prepared on a desktop publishing program, with a local Speedy Printing service providing the paper and printing, folding, stapling and tab-sealing for self-mailing. It usually consists of four pages printed front and back.

Our newsletter has been produced for nearly 9 years now... but other support groups can, and do, publish less elaborate and lengthy ones. Even if the newsletter is only 1 page, both sides, it can communicate very important information to readers, and can help even the most isolated patient to feel less alone.

In my experience with the Cape COPD Newsletters, I've found that it is good to strike a balance between information and support. Information might focus on something such as medicines or treatments, complimented with well-thought-out editorials addressing major emotional issues of lung disease, such as sporadic depression, coping skills to get you through the bad patches, achieving better understanding of the disease with your family members, and ways to help you get through the grieving process that results from the many losses of things you can no longer do.

The newsletters can also serve to keep members posted on news about other people in the group. Hospital stays, recuperations, deaths, and names of people who have graduated from or finished a pulmonary rehabilitation program, can all serve to draw members closer together and to encourage a bonding as a group. I frequently include a special article featuring a specific member, interviewing them in detail so that the group can get to know them better. People with lung disease often have led very interesting lives... many have traveled the world, some had positions of great authority with large companies, and some have fascinating hobbies and interests that they continue to presently enjoy. Butchers, bakers, candlestick makers—all of great interest to the other members of the support group.

Another important role of the newsletter is the contact that it provides for those people who are too sick to come to the meetings. They can still feel very much a part of the group each time the newsletter arrives in the mail for them. Since lung patients fight fatigue most of the time, and distressed breathing may discourage them from wanting to get dressed and go out, the newsletters may also serve to entice folks to *want to come to the meetings,* even at the price of feeling exhausted and overwhelmed by the illness. Most of them find that it is worth the extra effort they have to expend just to get there, and that they benefit enormously from the camaraderie and spirit of a group of people who can fully empathize with their plight.

It is good to encourage support group members to keep their copies of the newsletters. That way they can build their own personal file of information about lung disease... and be able to refer back to it later down the line, should they have a need for it. A simple 3-ring binder works well to hold and file the issues, filed by date.

⤙ The Meetings ⤚

By alternating the meetings between speakers and inter-active discussion formats, a lively pace can be kept up year to year. There are so many subjects of interest to lung patients that an unending list of speaker subjects can exist. *Some are: pulmonologists to speak on the specific subjects of COPD (emphysema/chronic bronchitis and/or bronchial asthma), bronchiectasis, pulmonary fibrosis or sarcoidosis, pulmonary hypertension or pulmonary embolisms, etc.; respiratory therapists to discuss and teach proper breathing exercises; physical therapists to present the importance of rehab programs and ongoing exercise; nutritionists; alterna-tive healing specialists; pharmacists re: medications; cardiologists to discuss the effects of lung disease on the entire respiratory system; fire department paramedics to cover the topic of what to do in case of an emergency.*

On the meeting days that are scheduled as interactive discussion groups, there are a number of ways to get the meetings off to a good start. If the group isn't too large, it's great to start off by letting each person introduce themselves and tell a brief synopsis of their history with lung illness. The stories that emerge may be similar or very different, but they seem to always be of interest to the other people in the room. This opening activity usually leads to active participa-tion and a more open discussion of issues. A two-hour meeting goes by very quickly.

Another jump-starter is to choose a subject for discus-sion and open it up to the natural give-and-take of a topic of mutual interest. 'Coping skills' is a good example... every-one who has lung disease has devised their own way around certain problems, or has learned to compensate for an activity that is no longer a viable choice. Someone in the group may be seeking a solution for a specific illness-related problem and many people in the room will offer suggestions to help them. Some members share examples of their own inventiveness. It is amazing how the room will sometimes ring with laughter, illustrating the group's need to maintain humor in their lives. Sometimes the laughter itself is the best solution.

There are other times when the discourse takes a turn toward sadness, which is hard to avoid when everyone in the group has a chronic illness. One person might be expressing their frustration over the compromises in their lifestyle now, or the disturbing effect of realizing that your disease is spiraling down faster than you had expected. During those times, tears will be shed... but they will be shed in good faith together, as friends who fully empathize with the situation. When these meetings are over, many of the attendees will express that they feel lighter, more optimistic, just for having shared their feelings with people who understand. No one seems embarrassed by the flow of tears.

An important consideration regarding meetings is the physical comfort of those in attendance. We discovered early on that our meetings flowed better when people were seated at long tables, giving them someplace to rest their arms and ease their breathing. We often set the meetings up in a U-shape, with the coordinator in the center of the U. Chairs can be placed on all sides of the tables, but it works best when the long tables are joined together end-to-end. This arrangement helps to set newcomers at ease, and to encourage active dialogue for discussions. In fact, the din of conversations may become overwhelming, calling for the necessity of a small bell or chime to bring attention back to whomever is speaking. This enthusiastic sharing of information is good, but at the same time, it is much more effective to keep the focus of talk and exchange where everyone can hear and only one dialogue is going on at one time.

Coffee or tea can be served or available on a help-yourself basis, as a hot drink serves well to open up clogged airways. It also promotes social exchange.

Group participation should be invited, even when a guest speaker is appearing. A Question and Answer session should follow every presentation, so that members can ask their own questions of the speaker. Additionally, evaluation sheets can be passed around for attendees to fill out after the program, grading or expressing their opinion on the quality of the speaker's presentation and the amount of information they were able to impart. We like to leave room on the sheet for members to fill in any topic on which they would like to hear a speaker. That way, they feel so much more a part of the group process.

⋙ Advisory Committees ⋘

Support groups, even though they are coordinated and run by individuals, should reflect the interests and involvement of all their members. One way to ensure that this happens is to form an Advisory Committee. Usually a selection of the most involved members, or volunteers, make up this committee along with the coordinator. Meetings are held several times each year to plan programs and speakers, and to address issues like fundraising and special projects.

This team will provide input on all things concerning the support group, and will help the coordinator whenever it is needed. They make a wonderful sounding board for any new concerns or issues. The entire membership should be made aware of the committee's identity, and encouraged to take any concerns regarding the support group to any member of the Advisory Committee. When major decisions are made that affect the whole group, it is wise to make it known that the Advisory Committee reviewed the issue with the coordinator, agreed upon it, and voted to go forward with it. It takes some of the heat off of the coordinator, and also helps the membership feel that their interests are being democratically represented.

People can serve on the Advisory Committee for any specified length of time that is agreeable to the group. They may either be appointed, voted in, or automatically accepted for a term if they have volunteered.

⟩⟩⟩ Attendance ⟨⟨⟨

Support groups may number from three to virtually any number of members and/or attendees. Attendance will probably not ever reflect 100% of the membership, because so many lung disease people are too ill to come. Our Cape COPD group averages 40 to 50 people at each monthly meeting. Most of the people attending are members, with a few spouses, care givers and interested professionals joining in. (We have respiratory therapists who come regularly, representing three or four of our oxygen supplier companies. Plus we are fortunate to have a pulmonary nurse who retired recently, and she has become active with our group, just to keep her hand in.)

It should be expected that, in bad or inclement, weather, attendance will be way down. People with lung disease are reluctant to venture out in very cold or stormy conditions. But, in general, they are a heartier group than one might suppose, showing up for most meetings regardless of the weather.

They will stay away, though, if they are sick or have a cold or virus. They respect the fragility of each other's situation, knowing that it is unwise to subject any lung patient to unnecessary infections. If they would use as much good judgment in opting not to be around their grandchildren when the kids bring home colds or flu, there would be many less exacerbations to report on.

∼ The Most Important Role ∼

The most important role for lung support groups is that of letting patients know that they are not alone in their suffering and grief. People will take comfort in knowing that others are worse off than they are, and that it is possible to manage life with the illness. Members will gain emotional support and strength from learning that there are things they can do to help themselves live more successfully and fully in spite of the disease. Their self-esteem will rise and will flourish as they bond and become involved with the other members. They might even be easier to live with, having learned that they aren't the only ones to feel the stigma of having to ask for help occasionally. They can become far less judgmental of their spouses and other family members, knowing that most people with lung disease suffer through the same kinds of misunderstandings.

Very importantly, members of support groups can find enormous encouragement by learning that *the bad days will pass,* and better times will present again. They learn this lesson well, by being able to greet each other time after time, at meeting after meeting. No other system or coping methodology will accomplish this objective for lung patients better or faster, or more consistently, than support groups.

Finally, here is a letter from the family of a member of the Cape Cod COPD Support Group, to Jo-Von.

Dear Jo-Von,

Nothing...enhanced my Mother's living more than the support and love and spiritual boost that she received from you and from the Cape COPD Support Group.

Once she immersed herself in COPD meetings and the concerns of others, her own maladies took a back seat. She focused on how to deal with COPD and invested her efforts toward how she might make things better for Ellie, Phyllis, Sam and Jo-Von.

You were an inspiration to her and so, you are an inspiration for me. I will never forget your kindness or your love for Mom or the effect that this wonderful synergy of friends and support had on her. In my Mother you had a devoted friend who rooted each day for your book to be published and then each day she rooted for a best seller!

She so supported you and your efforts. And this made the Cape COPD Support Group the one and only choice for our selection for donations to be made in her memory. With our best wishes for the work you do, with gratitude from a family who loved her, we enclose, also, our piece for COPD.

Thanks for everything, Jo-Von, with love from all of the Norgeots.

Sincerely,

Marc and Lorraine Norgeot, with fond regards from Skip Norgeot.

Jo-Von Tucker with oxygen and lobster

Reprinted by permission of Nellcor Puritan Bennett, Inc., Pleasanton, CA.

"Ultimately, we learn more from each other than from other sources."

John Walsh

➣ Parting Thoughts ⬌

In her book *The Chronic Illness Experience*, Cheri Register says, "Chronic illness is at the same time a personal misfortune and a sign of progress. Earlier and more precise diagnosis, more effective remedies against acute problems, and better means of maintaining health have slowed the course and limited the impact of some diseases that used to be quickly terminal. No long illnesses to *die of*, but still not thoroughly curable, they have become illnesses to *live with*."

"How well people manage lives marked by illness depends not on the nature of the illness but on the strength of their conviction that life is worth living no matter what complications are imposed on it."

The field of medicine is most concerned with keeping people alive. More recently and fortunately progress is being made in recognizing the value of helping patients achieve a higher level of physical function. But those who live within bodies with chronic disease are likely at some point— perhaps at many different points in time along the way—to go farther than the physical, asking, *"What is life for?"* For each person the answer is different, but perhaps in reading these stories you have had some help in finding your answer.

My hope for each of you is to find a way within your heart to know this, something once said by a person with a terminal illness: *"It's not all about being sick. It's all about living."* To love and to laugh often, to help yourself so that you are able to share of yourself to help others, and to live life to the fullest with happiness and joy. I wish for you to reach, and trust that you will find a way to grace yourself with the gift of truly living. Breathe better, live in wellness.

Glossary

Acute: An illness which comes on suddenly or very recently, within the last few hours or days.

Airway Obstruction: A blocking or narrowing of the airways on their way to or within the lung.

Alpha-1 Antitrypsin Deficiency: A hereditary disease in which there is not enough of a particular protective substance of the lungs. Patients with Alpha-1 Antitrypsin Deficiency develop severe emphysema in their 20's, 30's and 40's.

Alveoli: Tiny, sac-like structures at the ends of the airways where oxygen and carbon dioxide exchange take place.

Antibiotic: A drug that kills or inhibits bacteria.

Apnea: The absence of breathing, usually longer than 10 seconds. Obstructive sleep apnea is when a person periodically stops breathing during sleep due to an obstruction in the airway. Central sleep apnea is when, for some reason, the respiratory center in the brain fails to send the message to breathe.

Arterial Blood Gas (ABG): A blood test drawn from the artery to determine how well the lungs are working relative to other metabolic functions of the body.

Asthma: An obstructive lung disease characterized by airway hyper-responsiveness, inflammation, narrowing and spasm.

Asthmatic Bronchitis: A type of bronchitis commonly associated with COPD involving cough, airway hyper-responsiveness, and mucous production.

Bacteria: Infectious organisms that may produce bronchitis or pneumonia.

BiPAP: (Bi-level - inspiratory and expiratory - Positive Airway Pressure) A mechanical device used to assist breathing in severe lung disease, following surgery, or in obstructive sleep apnea. This treatment is "non-invasive", meaning that no tube is inserted into the lungs. Pressure is applied to the airways via a mask that can be quite easily and quickly put on and removed.

Bleb: Destroyed, non-functional part of the lung that takes up space and puts pressure on a less damaged portion of the lung.

Bronchial Hygiene: Keeping the lungs free of excess mucous by using inhalers, nebulizer treatments, percussion and postural drainage, effective cough techniques or other devices that aid in airway clearance.

Bronchitis: Irritation of the lining of the bronchial tubes, characterized by a frequent cough.

Bronchiectasis: Chronic infection often in the lower parts of the lung characterized by copious amounts of excess mucous.

Bronchus: The two main divisions from the trachea, each one leading into a lung. There are about 20 more sets of branches before reaching the alveoli, where oxygen and carbon dioxide exchange take place.

Chronic: Illness that has been present for a longer period of time, usually months or years.

Cilia: Hairlike structures that line the airways and sweep mucous upward toward the mouth. The cilia are important to cleanse the lungs and defend against irritants. Cilia can be destroyed by cigarette smoke and pollution.

Cor Pulmonale: Strain of the right side of the heart due to lung disease.

CPAP: (Continuous Positive Airway Pressure) A mechanical device used to assist breathing and in the treatment of obstructive sleep apnea. This treatment is "non-invasive", meaning that no tube is inserted into the lungs. Pressure is applied to the airways via a mask that can be quite easily and quickly put on and removed.

Diaphragm: The main muscle of breathing. The diaphragm is a large sheet of muscle separating the chest and the abdomen.

Dyspnea: Difficulty breathing, Shortness of Breath.

Emphysema: Destruction or enlargement of the alveoli.

Exacerbation: An episodic worsening of a chronic illness.

FEV $_1$: Forced Expiratory Volume in the first second of exhalation in a Pulmonary Function Test. Can be helpful in determining the degree of airway obstruction.

Inflammation: Irritated, reddened, and swollen tissue.

Metabolism: The consumption of nutrients combined with oxygen which produces energy and maintains living tissue.

Nebulizer: A breathing treatment in which liquid medication is made into a fine mist to be inhaled into the lungs. Can be taken in a medical facility or at home.

Pneumonia: A common infection in people with COPD caused by bacteria or virus.

Pneumothorax: Lung collapse causing air to leak from within the lung into the space between the lung and the chest wall, causing pain and difficulty breathing.

Pulmonary Fibrosis: A scarring and/or stiffening of the lung tissue, often manifesting itself in a decreased ability to transport oxygen into the bloodstream. Frequently the cause of this disorder is unknown.

Pulmonary Function Test: Various measurements of the ability to move air in and out of the lungs and exchange oxygen. Can be done in a complete or abbreviated form depending upon information required by the physician.

Pulse Oximeter: A device used to determine the percent of oxygen saturation in the blood. This test is non-invasive (nothing is placed inside the body), painless, and quickly and easily done.

Pursed Lips Breathing: A method of breathing which prolongs the expiratory phase, increasing the amount of carbon dioxide expelled, slowing down breathing and allowing the person using this method to gain more control over breathing.

Respiratory Failure: A chronic or acute state in which the lungs are unable to provide enough oxygen to the body and/or remove enough carbon dioxide from the body.

Silicosis: A respiratory disease caused by the inhalation of silica dust. When crystalline silica (a component of silica dust) is inhaled, it causes inflammation of the lung tissue. This inflammation leads to scar tissue formation on the lungs, also known as nodules, which obstructs the flow of oxygen into the lungs and into the bloodstream.

Sleep Study: A study done to observe various physiologic changes during sleep. Done overnight in a laboratory.

SOB: Short of Breath

Spirometer: A device used to measure lung function.

Trachea: The main airway leading to both lungs. Sometimes referred to as the windpipe.

Transtracheal Catheter: A small tube inserted into a hole in the trachea supplying oxygen to the lungs. Used for long term supplemental oxygen use in which a higher flow is required and / or if the patient does not wish to have a nasal cannula visible.

Ventilator: A mechanical device used to treat respiratory failure. Tubing from the ventilator is connected to an endotracheal tube inserted into the patient's lungs via the mouth or nose. Mechanical ventilation is considered to be an invasive treatment, meaning that something is inserted into the body. Also referred to as a respirator, but ventilator is the more proper term.

Virus: A group of highly contagious infectious agents causing a variety of head colds and chest infections. Antibiotics are ineffective against viruses. Vaccination against the influenza virus (flu shot) is effective.

Wheeze: A whistling sound of air entering or leaving the lungs. Can be a sign of muscle spasm around the airways, commonly found in asthma.

Resources

Books

The Chronic Illness Experience. Register, 1987, Hazelden Information and Educational Services.

Chronic Obstructive Pulmonary Disease. Jenkins.1999, Hazelen.

Courage and Inspiration for Life With Chronic Obstructive Pulmonary Disease. Carter, Nicotra, Tucker. 1999, New Technology Publishing, Inc.
To order: Jo-Von Tucker (508) 945-7771.

The Lung Transplantation Handbook. Couture. 2001, Trafford Publishing, Victoria, B.C., Canada.

Enjoying Life With COPD. Petty and Nett, 1995, Laennec Publishing, Inc.

Taking Flight: Inspirational Stories of Lung Transplantation. Schum. 2002, Trafford Publishing, Victoria, B.C., Canada.

A more complete selection of helpful books and materials can be found at the Breathing Better, Living Well Bookstore at: www.Breathingbetterlivingwell.com

Organizations

Allergy and Asthma Network /
Mothers of Asthmatics, Inc.
2751 Prosperity Ave.
Suite 150
Fairfax, VA 22031-4397
1-800-878-4403
1-703-641-9595
fax: 1-703-573-7794
website: www.aanma.org
email: aanma@aol.com

Alpha-1 National Association
8120 Penn Ave., South
Suite 549
Minneapolis, MN 55431-1326
1-800-521-3025
website: www.alpha1.org

Alpha-1 Foundation
2937 S. W. 27th Ave.
Suite 302
Miami, FL 33133
1-888-825-7421
1-305-567-9888
fax: 1-305-567-1317
website: www.alphaone.org

American Association for Cardiovascular and
Pulmonary Rehabilitation
7611 Elmwood Ave.
Suite 201
Middleton, WI 53562
1-608-831-6989
website: www.aacvpr.org

American Lung Association
1740 Broadway
New York, NY 10019
1-800-LUNG-USA
1-800-586-4872
website: www.lungusa.org

Asthma and Allergy Foundation of America
1125 15th St., N.W.
Suite 502
Washington, DC 20005
1-800-727-8462

Better Breathers Club

Check with your local hospital or the American Lung Association.
1-800-LUNG-USA
www.lungusa.org

California Thoracic Society
202 Fashion Lane, Suite 219
Tustin, CA 92780-3320
Phone: 714-730-1944
Fax: 714-730-4057
ctslung@aol.com
www.thoracic.org/ca.html

Cape Cod Support Group
c/o Clambake Celebrations
1223 Main Street
Chatham, MA 02633
1-508-945-7771
email: clambabe@capecod.net

CareSsentials, Inc.
347 Abington Road
Encinitas, CA 92024-4205
(760) 436-5064 voice
(760) 634-6989 fax
Info@CareSsentials.com
www.caressentials.com

Cheshire Medical Center
580-590 Court St.
Keene, NH 03431
1-603-354-5400
www.cheshire-med.com

Coalition for Pulmonary Fibrosis
1685 Branham Ln. Ste. 227
San Jose, CA 95118
1-888-222-8541
website: www.coalitionforpf.org
email: info@coalitionforpf.org

The National Jewish Medical and Research Center
1400 Jackson St.
Denver, CO 80206
1-303-388-4461
1-800-222-LUNG
website: www.njh.org

National Emphysema/COPD Association (NECA)
P.O. Box 11725
Kimberly Square Station
Albany, NY 12211-0725
www.COPDcommunity.org

Pulmonary Education and Research Foundation
Second Wind Newsletter
PERF
P.O. Box 1133
Lomita, CA 90717-5133
1-310-539-8390
website: www.perf2ndwind.org
e-mail: perf@pacbell.net

Well Spouse Foundation
30 East 40th St. suite PH
New York, NY 10016
(212) 685-8815
www.wellspouse.org

Additional Resources Online

www.aaaai.org
American Academy of Allergy, Asthma, and Immunology

www.aanma.org
Allergy and Asthma Network / Mothers of Asthmatics

www.aarc.org
The American Association for Respiratory Care

www.alphanet.org
A not-for-profit disease management company

www.alphaone.org
Alpha-One Foundation

www.alphaoneregistry.org
Alpha-1 carriers are encouraged to join this confidential
research registry.

www.asthma.org.uk/
National Asthma Campaign

www.breatheinfo.com
Astra Zeneca Pharmaceuticals

www.breethezy.com
Practical techniques for living with mechanical ventilation

www.buyersguide.aarc.org

www.breathingbetterlivingwell.com
Recognizing the Emotional Aspects of Chronic Lung
Disease
janemartin@breathingbetterlivingwell.com

www.thoracic.org/ca.html
California Thoracic Society

www.caressentials.com
CareSsentials, Inc.

www.caringbridge.com
Communicating with friends and family online during an
illness or medical procedure

www.coalitionforpf.org
Coalition for Pulmonary Fibrosis

www.coloradohealthsite.org

www.COPD-International.com
COPD International (formerly Bill Horden's website)

www.copd-support.com
COPD on-line support group

www.dallasasthma.org
Dallas Asthma Consortium

www.emphysema.net
EFFORTS (Emphysema Foundation for our Right to
Survive)

www.goldcopd.com

www.HealthyResources.com
Information on COPD and Sleep Apnea

www.ibreathe.com
Glaxo Smith Kline Pharmaceuticals

www.liverfoundation.org
American Liver Foundation

www.lungusa.org
The American Lung Association

www.njh.org
National Jewish Hospital
www.nhlbi.nih.gov/health/public/lung/other/copd/index.htm
Information on COPD

http://www.nhlbi.nih.gov/health/prof/lung/nett/lvrsweb.htm
National Emphysema Treatment Trial (NETT)

www.nlhep.org
National Lung Health Education Program (NLHEP)
email: NLHEP@aol.com

www.oxyten4travel.com
Breathin' Easy Travel Guide

www.papapoo.com
Personal stories of life with COPD

www.perf2ndwind.org
Pulmonary Education and Research Foundation (PERF)

www.pulmonaryfibrosisassn.com

www.Pulmonarypaper.org
Newsletter for patients and families with Chronic Lung
Disease

www.2ndwind.org
Information and resources about lung transplant

www.thebreathingspace.com
Boehringer-Ingelheim Pharmaceuticals

www.uscopd.com
US COPD Coalition

www.wellspouse.org
Well Spouse Foundation

Index

Jane M. Martin

Jane M. Martin is a respiratory therapist with over twenty years of experience working in the acute care and outpatient settings. She founded and currently coordinates the Better Breathers' Club and the Pulmonary Rehab program at the Holland Community Hospital. Jane has written and spoken extensively on ways to improve pulmonary care across the patient continuum, as well as on the value of emotional support for improving the quality of life for pulmonary patients. Her featured articles have appeared in various regional and national publications. Jane was selected as the first author to participate in Infinity Publishing's *Authors Who Make A Difference* program based on her insightful book <u>Breathe Better, Live in Wellness: Winning Your Battle Over Shortness of Breath</u>. Originally from the Chicago area, she graduated with from Hope College with a B.A. in education and language arts. She received her respiratory degree while working with people with pulmonary disease, going on to develop educational programs for patients and the community. Jane lives in Holland, Michigan with her husband and two children.

Special Discount Offer for Pulmonary Groups from Infinity Publishing

Infinity Publishing's *Authors Who Make A Difference* program makes it possible for Better Breathers' Clubs, other pulmonary support groups, and Pulmonary Rehabilitation programs to purchase copies of this book directly from the publisher. These groups may order <u>Breathe Better, Live in Wellness</u> at 50% off the cover price of $17.95 for just $8.98 per book when six or more copies are ordered at the same time by the group leader. This is Infinity's way of reaching out to help folks who will benefit the most from this book as well as demonstrating that we are a publisher that is, indeed, making a difference.

This special discount of 50% off the cover price is only available when the group leader places the order by calling Infinity Publishing's toll-free phone number:

877-BUY-BOOK   (877-289-2665)

We accept all major credit cards. All book orders are shipped promptly within 24 to 48 hours, and when you order 20 copies or more, Infinity will pay the shipping charges to any destination in the continental U.S..

Individual orders at the cover price may be placed by calling 877-289-2665 or through our online bookstore at:

www.buybooksontheweb.com

Infinity Publishing's just-in-time book publishing system makes book sponsorship easy and efficient. Digitally printed books can include an up-to-date sponsorship page as well as the sponsor's logo on the cover. Book sponsorship is the perfect way to get your message into the hands of your customers and / or conference participants. Many of our authors are available for autographing appearances.

A minimum order of 100 books, along with a nominal set-up fee, is required for sponsorship. Entering into an agreement to order 500 or more books each month earns a discount of 55% off the cover price. Organizations may order as few or as many books needed to have on hand or for a sponsored event. Infinity Publishing pays shipping and can send books directly to your office or conference location. Sponsorships are non-exclusive and sponsored books are not returnable.

We would be delighted to send you two complimentary copies of any qualified Infinity titles you may be interested in sponsoring. Five or more copies may be ordered at 40% off the cover price and, as always, whenever 20 or more books are ordered, Infinity pays shipping. Automatic shipment and monthly billing are available through our sponsorship program. Please contact our office at 1-877-BUY-BOOK for more information. We look forward to talking with you soon.